Christmas

AT THAT PATCHWORK PLACE

Martingale™
& COMPANY

Christmas at That Patchwork Place
© 2001 by Martingale & Company™

 *Martingale*™
& COMPANY

That Patchwork Place® is an imprint of Martingale & Company.

Martingale & Company
20205 144th Ave. NE
Woodinville, WA 98072-8478
www.martingale-pub.com

Printed in China

06 05 04 03 02 01 8 7 6 5 4 3 2

Library of Congress Cataloging-in-Publication Data

Christmas quilts at That Patchwork Place.
    p. cm.
    ISBN 1-56477-380-9
      1. Patchwork—Patterns. 2. Quilting—Patterns.
    3. Patchwork quilts. 4. Christmas decorations.
    I. That Patchwork Place, Inc.

TT835 .C493 2001
746.46'041–dc21

2001022250

Mission Statement

We are dedicated to providing quality products and service by working together to inspire creativity and to enrich the lives we touch.

CREDITS

President: Nancy J. Martin
CEO: Daniel J. Martin
Publisher: Jane Hamada
Editorial Director: Mary V. Green
Editorial Project Manager: Tina Cook
Technical Editor: Dawn Anderson

Copy Editor: Karen Koll
Design and Production Manager: Stan Green
Illustrator: Laurel Strand
Cover Designer: Rohani Design
Text Designer: Regina Girard
Photographer: Brent Kane

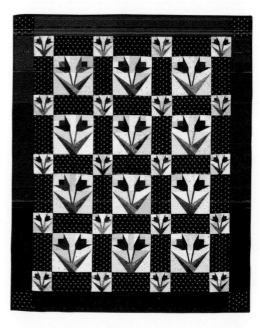

Contents

Introduction

A Christmas quilt has a way of magically filling a room with all the warmth and comfort the holidays have to offer. Bits of red and green fabrics stitched into a dazzling display of color and texture can instantly sweep us back into that familiar world of shiny bows on boxes, glistening ornaments on trees, and powdery snow on sidewalks. The quilts we make especially to showcase on a wall or cuddle under each Christmas remind us to enjoy every moment of this special time of year, which quickly arrives and even more quickly is gone.

Whether your favorite Christmas memories stem from the season's more traditional symbols or the lighter side of the holidays, there's a project here to delight you (and those lucky enough to be on your gift list). Sparkling snowflakes, whimsical snowmen, poinsettias, holly, and classic stars are just a few of the much-loved motifs you'll enjoy stitching in anticipation of the chilly winter months.

The quilts in this book come from some of America's most popular designers, including That Patchwork Place® authors Roxanne Carter, Mimi Dietrich, Vicki Garnas, Amy Whalen Helmkamp, Tricia Lund, Deborah J. Moffett-Hall, Judy Pollard, and Retta Warehime. We hope you'll be inspired by their love of Christmas and enjoy giving their creations your own personal touch.

You're sure to find your technique of choice within these pages, from easy rotary cutting to precise paper piecing and portable hand appliqué. And if you're new to quiltmaking, there's a complete, step-by-step section on basic techniques that will walk you through each stage of the process.

So, if you're ever in need of gift ideas for friends and family, a special contribution to your favorite charity, or a quilt to enjoy each year in your own home, just turn these pages. *Christmas at That Patchwork Place* is sure to inspire the Christmas spirit in you for many seasons to come.

Cardinals by Deborah J. Moffett-Hall.
See page 85 for instructions.

Quiltmaking Basics

Fabric

For best results, select high-quality, 100 percent–cotton fabrics. They hold their shape well and are easy to handle. Cotton blends can be more difficult to stitch and press. Sometimes, however, a cotton blend is worth a little extra effort if it is the perfect fabric for your quilt.

Yardage requirements for all the projects in this book are based on 42" of usable fabric after preshrinking. Some quilts call for an assortment of scraps. If you have access to scraps, feel free to use them and purchase only those fabrics you need to complete the quilt you are making.

Prewash all fabric to test for colorfastness and remove excess dye. Wash dark and light colors separately so that dark colors do not run onto light fabrics. Some fabrics may require several rinses to eliminate excess dyes. Press the fabric so you can cut out the pieces accurately.

Supplies

Marking Tools: Various tools are available to mark fabrics when tracing around templates or marking quilting lines. Use a sharp #2 pencil or fine-lead mechanical pencil on light-colored fabrics; use a silver or yellow marking pencil on dark fabrics. Chalk pencils or chalk-wheel markers also make clear marks on fabrics. Be sure to test your marking tool to make sure you can remove its marks easily.

Needles: For machine piecing, a size 70/10 or 80/12 works well for most cottons. For hand appliqué, choose a needle that will glide easily through the edges of the appliqué pieces. Size 10 (fine) to size 12 (very fine) needles work well.

Pins: Long, fine "quilter's" pins with glass or plastic heads are easy to handle. Small ½"- to ¾"-long sequin pins work well for appliqué.

Rotary-Cutting Tools: You will need a rotary cutter, cutting mat, and clear acrylic rulers in a variety of sizes, including 6" x 6", 6" x 24", 12" x 12", and 15" x 15".

Scissors: Use your best scissors to cut fabric only. Use an older pair of scissors to cut paper, cardboard, and template plastic. Small, 4" scissors are handy for clipping threads.

Seam Ripper: Use this tool to remove stitches from incorrectly sewn seams.

Sewing Machine: To machine piece, you'll need a sewing machine that has a good straight stitch. You'll also need a walking foot or darning foot if you are going to machine quilt.

Template Plastic: Use clear or frosted plastic (available at quilt shops) to make durable, accurate templates.

Thread: Use good-quality, all-purpose cotton thread or cotton-covered polyester thread.

Rotary Cutting

The projects in this book include instructions for quick-and-easy rotary cutting wherever possible. All measurements include standard ¼"-wide seam allowances. For those unfamiliar with rotary cutting, a brief introduction is provided below. For more detailed information, see Donna Thomas's *Shortcuts: A Concise Guide to Rotary Cutting* (That Patchwork Place, 1999).

1. Fold the fabric and match selvages, aligning the crosswise and lengthwise grains as much as possible. Place the folded edge closest to you on the cutting mat. Align a square ruler along the folded edge of the fabric; then place a long, straight ruler to the left of the square ruler, just covering the uneven raw edges on the left side of the fabric. Remove the square ruler and cut along the right edge of the long ruler, rolling the rotary cutter away from you.

Discard the cut strip. (Reverse this procedure if you are left-handed.)

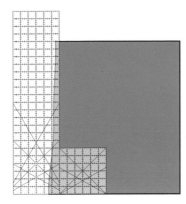

2. To cut strips, align the required measurements on the ruler with the newly cut edge of the fabric. For example, to cut a 2½"-wide strip, place the 2½" ruler mark on the edge of the fabric.

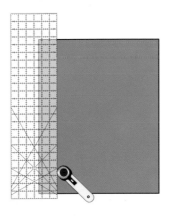

3. To cut squares, cut strips in the required widths. Trim away the selvage ends of the strip. Align the required measurement on the ruler with the left edge of the strip and cut a square. Continue cutting squares until you have the number needed.

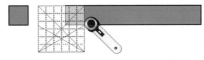

Half-Square Triangles
Make half-square triangles by cutting a square in half on the diagonal. The triangle's short sides are on the straight grain of fabric.

1. Cut squares to the finished measurement of the triangle's short sides plus ⅞" for seam allowances.

2. Stack squares and cut once diagonally, corner to corner. Each square yields 2 triangles.

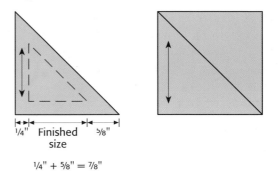

Quarter-Square Triangles
Make quarter-square triangles by cutting a square in quarters on the diagonal. The triangle's long side is on the straight grain of fabric.

1. Cut squares to the finished measurement of the triangle's long side plus 1¼" for seam allowances.

2. Stack squares and cut twice diagonally, corner to corner. Each square yields 4 triangles.

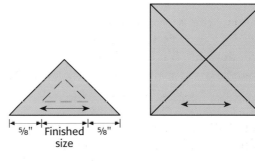

Machine Piecing

Sewing Accurate Seam Allowances
For machine piecing, it is important to maintain a consistent ¼"-wide seam allowance. Otherwise, the quilt blocks will not be the desired finished size, which in turn affects the size of everything else in the quilt, including alternate blocks, sashings, and borders. Measurements for all parts for

each quilt include ¼" on each edge for seam allowances.

Establish an exact ¼"-wide seam guide on your machine. Some machines have a special foot that measures exactly ¼" from the center needle position to the edge of the foot. This feature allows you to use the edge of the presser foot to guide the fabric for a perfect ¼"-wide seam allowance. If your machine doesn't have such a foot, create a seam guide by placing the edge of a piece of tape or moleskin ¼" from the needle.

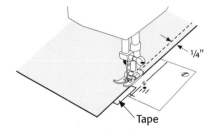

Tape

Easing

If two pieces that will be sewn together are slightly different in size (less than ⅛" difference), pin the places where the two pieces should match and in the middle, if necessary, to distribute the excess fabric evenly. Sew the seam with the longer piece on the bottom. The feed dogs will ease the two pieces together.

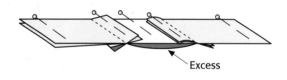

Excess

Pressing

The traditional rule in quiltmaking is to press seams to one side, toward the darker color wherever possible. Press the seam flat from the wrong side first, and then press the seam in the desired direction from the right side. Press carefully to avoid distorting the shapes. Press the seams in the direction of the arrows in accompanying illustrations unless otherwise noted.

When joining two seamed units, plan ahead and press the seam allowances in opposite directions as shown to reduce bulk and make it easier to

match seam lines. Where two seams meet, the seam allowances will butt against each other, making it easier to join units with perfectly matched seam intersections.

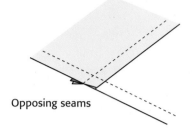

Opposing seams

Basic Appliqué

Instructions are provided for several appliqué methods, including needle-turn appliqué, freezer paper appliqué, and fusible appliqué.

Making Templates

Make your appliqué templates from clear plastic; it is more durable and accurate than cardboard. Since you can see through the plastic, it is easy to trace the templates accurately.

Place template plastic over each pattern piece and trace with a fine-line permanent marker. Do not add seam allowances. Cut out the templates on the drawn lines. Mark the pattern name and grain-line arrow (if applicable) on the template.

Traditional Appliqué Stitch

The traditional appliqué stitch or blind stitch is appropriate for sewing all appliqué shapes, including sharp points and curves.

1. Tie a knot in a single strand of thread approximately 18" long.

2. Hide the knot by slipping the needle into the seam allowance from the wrong side of the appliqué piece, bringing it out on the fold line.

3. Work from right to left if you are right-handed, or left to right if you are left-handed. Start the first stitch by moving the needle straight off the appliqué, inserting the needle

into the background fabric. Let the needle travel under the background fabric, parallel to the edge of the appliqué, bringing it up about ⅛" away, along the pattern line.

4. As you bring the needle up, pierce the edge of the appliqué piece, catching only one or two threads of the folded edge.

5. Move the needle straight off the appliqué into the background fabric. Let your needle travel under the background, bringing it up about ⅛" away, again catching the edge of the appliqué.

6. Give the thread a slight tug and continue stitching.

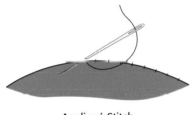

Appliqué Stitch

7. To end your stitching, pull the needle through to the wrong side. Behind the appliqué piece, take two small stitches, making knots by taking your needle through the loops.

8. If desired, trim the background fabric that lies under each appliqué piece to reduce the bulk and make it easier to quilt. Turn the block over and make a tiny cut in the background fabric. Trim the fabric ¼" away from the stitching line, being careful not to cut through the appliquéd piece.

Needle-Turn Appliqué

1. Using a plastic template, trace the design onto the right side of the appliqué fabric. Use a #2 pencil on light fabrics; use a white or yellow pencil on dark fabrics.

2. Cut out the fabric piece, adding a scant ¼"-wide seam allowance all around.

3. Position the appliqué piece on the background fabric; pin or baste in place.

4. Starting on a straight edge, use the tip of the needle to gently turn under the seam allowance, about ½" at a time. Hold the turned seam allowance firmly between the thumb and first finger of your left hand (reverse if left-handed) as you stitch the appliqué to the background. Use a longer needle—a Sharp or a milliner's needle—to help you control the seam allowance and turn it under neatly. Use the traditional appliqué stitch described at left to sew your appliqué pieces to the background.

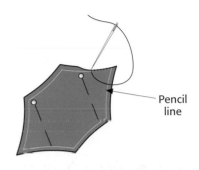

Pencil line

Reverse Appliqué

In reverse appliqué, you cut through a layer of fabric, turn under the edges, and stitch around them, using the traditional appliqué stitch in order to reveal a second layer of fabric. This technique was used on the door, windows, and hill of "Winter Solstice" on page 50.

1. Cut the top layer of fabric ¹⁄₁₆" from the appliqué edge or opening as indicated by the pattern. Clip any inside corners and curves. Insert bottom fabric piece under the opening, if necessary.

2. Following the instructions for needle-turn appliqué on page 9, turn under the raw edges and stitch in place.

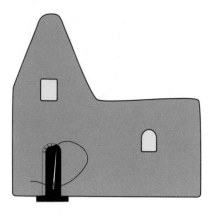

Freezer-Paper Appliqué

In freezer-paper appliqué, freezer-paper backing is used to stabilize the appliqué piece during the appliqué process. Then the backing fabric is cut away and the freezer paper is removed.

1. Trace the appliqué templates in reverse onto the unwaxed side of the freezer paper. Cut on the marked lines.

2. Fuse the freezer-paper templates, shiny side down, to the wrong side of the fabric. Use a dry iron and leave at least ¾" between pieces.

3. Cut around the freezer-paper templates, adding ¼" seam allowances. Clip inner curves, notch outer curves, and trim across outside corners.

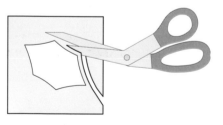

4. Fold the seam allowances over the freezer paper, securing with a fabric gluestick.

5. Place the appliqué on the background fabric and secure in place with a traditional appliqué stitch (see page 8). Cut away the background fabric from behind the appliqué, leaving a ¼"-wide seam allowance. Remove the freezer paper; spray lightly with water if necessary to loosen the bond. Press.

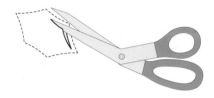

Fusible Appliqué

Fusible appliqué is a quick method of appliqué. The edges of the appliqué pieces can be covered with buttonhole stitching or with a ¼" bias strip, as in "Ruth's Bouquet" on page 75, or left exposed as for the berries on the "Cardinals" quilt on page 85.

1. Place fusible web, paper side up, over the appliqué pattern. Trace the reverse of the pattern onto the paper side of the web, tracing all pieces to be cut from the same fabric together and leaving about ¼" between the pieces. Cut around the group of appliqué pieces.

2. Place the marked fusible web on the wrong side of the appropriate fabric, paper side up. Fuse, following the manufacturer's directions.

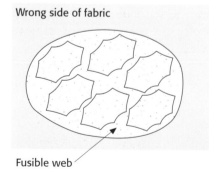

Wrong side of fabric

Fusible web

3. Cut out the pieces on the marked lines. Peel off the paper backing. Position the appliqués right side up on the quilt top. Fuse in place, following the manufacturer's directions.

Buttonhole Stitch

Use a buttonhole stitch around the outer edges of an appliqué for a decorative touch. The instructions below are for a hand-worked buttonhole stitch. You can also use a machine buttonhole stitch.

1. Thread the needle with 3 strands of 18"-long embroidery floss. Tie a knot at one end.

2. Pull the needle through the fabric at point A, next to the edge of the appliqué. Then insert the needle at point B and pull it through the fabric at point C. Repeat.

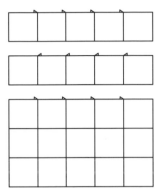

Assembling the Quilt Top

Squaring Up Blocks

After stitching your quilt blocks together, take the time to square them up. Use a large square ruler to measure your blocks and make sure they are the desired size plus an extra ¼" on each edge for seam allowances. For example, if you are making 6" blocks, they should all measure 6½" before you sew them together. If your blocks vary slightly in size, trim the larger blocks to match the size of the smallest block. Be sure to trim all four sides; otherwise, your block will be lopsided.

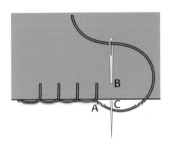

If your blocks are not the required finished size, you will have to adjust all the other components of the quilt accordingly.

Making Straight-Set Quilts

1. Arrange the blocks as shown in the diagram provided with each quilt.

2. Sew blocks together in horizontal rows; press the seams in opposite directions from row to row (unless directed otherwise).

3. Sew the rows together, making sure to match the seams between the blocks.

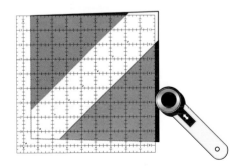

Straight-Set Quilts

Making Diagonally Set Quilts

1. Arrange the blocks, side triangles, and corner triangles as shown in the diagram provided with each quilt.

2. Sew the blocks together in diagonal rows; press the seams in opposite directions from row to row (unless directed otherwise).

3. Sew the rows together, making sure to match the seams between the blocks. Sew on the corner triangles last.

Note: Sometimes side and corner triangles are cut larger than necessary and trimmed later.

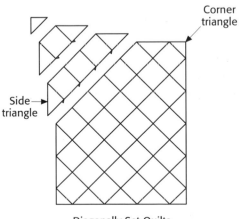

Diagonally Set Quilts

Adding Borders

For best results, do not cut border strips and sew them directly to the quilt sides without measuring first. The edges of a quilt often measure slightly longer than the distance through the quilt center, due to stretching during construction. Measure the quilt top through the center in both directions to determine how long to cut the border strips. This step ensures that the finished quilt will be as straight and as "square" as possible, without wavy edges.

Plain borders are commonly cut along the crosswise grain and seamed where extra length is needed. Borders cut from the lengthwise grain of fabric require extra yardage, but seaming to achieve the required length is then unnecessary.

Straight-Cut Borders

1. Measure the length of the quilt top through the center. Cut border strips to that measurement, piecing as necessary. Mark the center of the quilt edges and the border strips. Pin the border strips to the sides of the quilt top, matching the center marks and ends and easing as necessary. Sew the border strips in place. Press the seams toward the border.

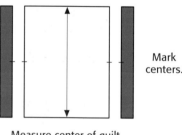

Measure center of quilt,
top to bottom.

2. Measure the width of the quilt top through the center, including the side border strips just added. Cut border strips to that measurement, piecing as necessary. Mark the center of the quilt edges and the border strips. Pin the border strips to the top and bottom edges of the quilt top, matching the center marks and

ends and easing as necessary; stitch. Press the seams toward the border.

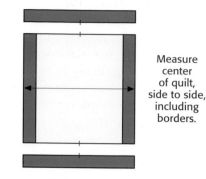

Measure center of quilt, side to side, including borders.

Mark centers.

Borders with Corner Squares

1. Measure the width and length of the quilt top through the center. Cut border strips to those measurements, piecing as necessary.

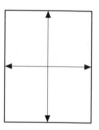

2. Mark the center of the quilt edges and the border strips. Pin the side border strips to opposite sides of the quilt top, matching centers and ends and easing as necessary. Sew the side border strips; press seams toward the border.

3. Cut corner squares the required size (the cut width of the border strips). Sew one corner square to each end of the remaining two border strips; press seams toward the border strips. Pin the border strips to the top and bottom edges of the quilt top. Match centers, seams between the border strip and corner squares, and ends, easing as necessary; stitch. Press seams toward the border.

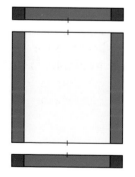

Preparing to Quilt

Marking the Quilting Lines

Whether or not to mark the quilting designs depends upon the type of quilting you will be doing. Marking is not necessary if you plan to quilt in the ditch, outline-quilt a uniform distance from seam lines, or free-motion quilt in a random pattern. For more complex quilting designs, mark the quilt top before the quilt is layered with batting and backing.

Choose a marking tool that will be visible on your fabric and test it on fabric scraps to be sure the marks can be removed easily. See "Marking Tools" on page 6 for options. Masking tape can also be used to mark straight quilting. Tape only small sections at a time and remove the tape when you stop at the end of the day; otherwise, the sticky residue may be difficult to remove from the fabric.

Layering the Quilt

The quilt "sandwich" consists of the backing, batting, and quilt top. Cut the quilt backing at least 4" larger than the quilt top all the way around. For large quilts, it is usually necessary to sew two or three lengths of fabric together to make a backing the required size. Trim away the selvages before piecing the lengths together. Press the backing seams open to make quilting easier.

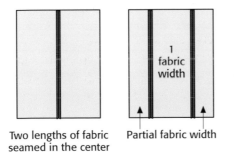

Two lengths of fabric seamed in the center   Partial fabric width

Batting comes packaged in standard bed sizes, or it can be purchased by the yard. Several weights or thicknesses are available. Thick battings are fine for tied quilts and comforters; a thinner batting is better if you intend to quilt by hand or machine.

To put it all together:

1. Spread the backing, wrong side up, on a flat, clean surface. Anchor it with pins or masking tape. Be careful not to stretch the backing out of shape.

2. Spread the batting over the backing, smoothing out any wrinkles.

3. Place the pressed quilt top, right side up, on top of the batting. Smooth out any wrinkles and make sure the edges of the quilt top are parallel to the edges of the backing.

4. Starting in the center, baste with needle and thread and work diagonally to each corner. Continue basting in a grid of horizontal and vertical lines 6" to 8" apart. Finish by basting around the edges.

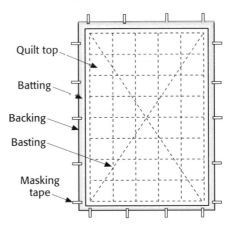

Note: For machine quilting, you may baste the layers with #2 rustproof safety pins. Place pins about 6" to 8" apart, away from the area you intend to quilt.

Quilting Techniques

Hand Quilting

To quilt by hand, you will need short, sturdy needles (called "Betweens"), quilting thread, and a thimble to fit the middle finger of your sewing hand. Most quilters also use a frame or hoop to support their work. Use the smallest needle you can comfortably handle; the finer the needle, the smaller your stitches will be.

1. Thread your needle with a single strand of quilting thread about 18" long; make a small knot and insert the needle in the top layer about 1" from the place where you want to start stitching. Pull the needle out at the point where quilting will begin and gently pull the thread until the knot pops through the fabric and into the batting.

2. Take small, evenly spaced stitches through all three quilt layers.

3. Rock the needle up and down through all layers until you have 3 or 4 stitches on the needle. Place your other hand underneath the quilt so you can feel the needle point with the tip of your finger when you take a stitch.

4. To end a line of quilting, make a small knot close to the last stitch; then backstitch, running the thread a needle's length through the batting. Gently pull the thread until the knot pops into the batting; clip the thread at the quilt's surface.

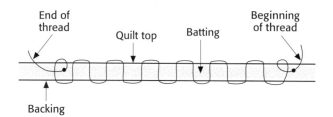

Machine Quilting

Machine quilting is suitable for all types of quilts, from crib quilts to full-size bed quilts. With machine quilting, you can quickly complete quilts that might otherwise languish on the shelves.

For straight-line quilting, it is extremely helpful to have a walking foot to help feed the quilt layers through the machine without shifting or puckering. Some machines have a built-in walking foot; other machines require a separate attachment.

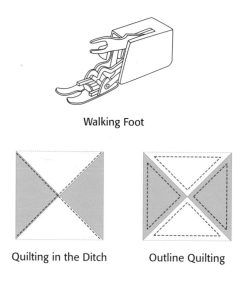

Walking Foot

Quilting in the Ditch   Outline Quilting

For free-motion quilting, you need a darning foot and the ability to drop the feed dogs on your machine. With free-motion quilting, you do not turn the fabric under the needle but instead guide the fabric in the direction of the design. Use free-motion quilting to outline-quilt a pattern in the fabric or to create stippling and many other curved designs.

Darning Foot

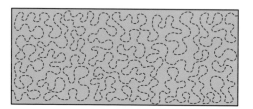

Free-Motion Quilting

Finishing

Binding

For a French double-fold binding, cut strips 2" wide. Cut strips across the width of the fabric. You will need enough strips to go around the perimeter of the quilt, plus 10" for seams and the corners in a mitered fold.

1. Sew strips, right sides together, to make one long piece of binding. Join the strips at right angles and stitch across the corner as shown. Trim excess fabric and press the seams open.

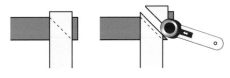

Joining Straight-Cut Strips

2. Fold the strip in half lengthwise, wrong sides together, and press. Trim one end of the strip at a 45° angle, turn under ¼", and press. Turning the end under at an angle distributes the bulk so you won't have a lump where the two ends of the binding meet.

Fold line

3. Trim the batting and backing even with the quilt top. If you plan to add a sleeve, do so now before attaching the binding.

4. Starting on one side of the quilt and using a ¼"-wide seam allowance, stitch the binding to the quilt, keeping the raw edges even with the quilt-top edge. End the stitching ¼" from the corner of the quilt and backstitch. Clip the thread.

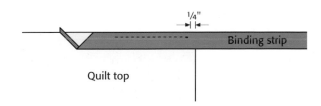

Quilt top
¼"
Binding strip

5. Turn the quilt so that you'll be stitching down the next side. Fold the binding up, away from the quilt, then back down onto itself, parallel with the edge of the quilt top. Begin stitching at the edge, backstitching to secure. Repeat on the remaining edges and corners of the quilt.

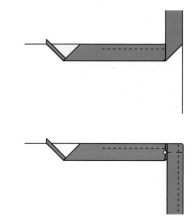

6. When you reach the beginning of the binding, overlap the beginning stitches by about 1" and cut away any excess binding, trimming the end at a 45° angle. Tuck the end of the binding into the fold and finish the seam.

7. Fold the binding over the raw edges of the quilt to the back, with the folded edge covering the row of machine stitching, and blindstitch in place. A miter will form at each corner. Blindstitch the mitered corners.

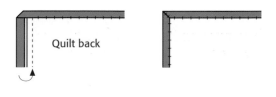

Quilt back

Signing Your Quilt

Future generations will want to know more than just who made your quilt and when. Labels can be as elaborate or as simple as you desire. You can write, type, or embroider the information. Be sure to include your name, the name of the quilt, your city and state, the date, the name of the recipient if it is a gift, and any other interesting or important information about the quilt.

Holly Wreaths

Holly Wreaths by Mimi Dietrich, 1984, Baltimore, Maryland, 41" x 41".

This traditional holly appliqué design is adapted from an antique album design given to Mimi by an appliqué teacher almost twenty years ago. The quilting design was inspired by a 1973 Christmas Memory pattern from Quilter's Newsletter Magazine.

Finished Block Size: 20" x 20"

Materials: *42"-wide fabric*

2½ yds. off-white fabric for appliqué background and backing

1¼ yd. green print for stems, holly leaves, and Prairie Points

⅜ yd. red print for berries and border

44" x 44" piece of batting

Cutting

From the off-white fabric, cut:

> 4 squares, 20½" x 20½", for appliqué background blocks

From the green print, cut:

> 4 bias strips, 1" x 30", for appliquéd stems
>
> 48 holly leaves for appliqué (see pattern on page 21)
>
> 92 squares, 3" x 3", for Prairie Points

From the red print, cut:

> 48 holly berries for appliqué (see pattern on page 21)
>
> 2 strips, 1" x 40½", for side border strips
>
> 2 strips, 1" x 41½", for top and bottom border strips

Appliquéing the Blocks

Note: You will need 4 appliquéd Holly Wreath blocks for this quilt. Follow the directions below to make each block. Refer to "Basic Appliqué" on pages 8–11 for general appliqué techniques.

1. Carefully press each 20½" background square in half and then in quarters; set aside. Trace or photocopy the pattern on page 21. Tape to a second piece of paper to make a 10" square pattern. Complete the dashed quilting lines for the wreath border, using the marked lines on the pattern as a guide. Place the background square over the pattern, aligning the center lines with the pressed crease lines; tape the pieces over a lightbox or sunny window. Lightly trace the solid lines onto the fabric with a fabric marking pencil. Repeat in each section to trace a total of 4 designs. Set aside.

2. Fold in ¼" to wrong side on long edges of each 1" x 30" green stem strip. Baste along the folded edges using small running stitches.

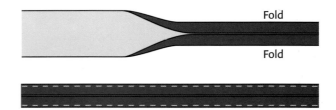

Gently pull up the basting stitches on one side to ease the strip into a curve.

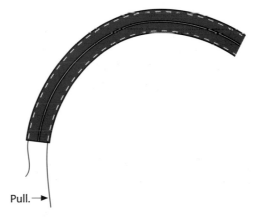

Pull.→

3. Pin the strip to the background square, positioning it on the marked stem lines. Appliqué in place (see "Traditional Appliqué Stitch" on page 8). When you get to the end, trim the edges so they overlap ½"; fold under ¼" on one end and overlap the raw edge on the remaining end. Finish appliquéing the stem in place.

Fold under ¼".

4. Appliqué 12 holly leaves traced from the pattern on page 21 to the background square (see "Freezer-Paper Appliqué" on page 10). Use the marked lines on the background as a guide for placement.

5. Trace the holly berry template pattern onto heavy paper; cut out. Pin the paper circle to the wrong side of the berry fabric and cut ¼" from the outer edge of the paper. Baste a running stitch ⅛" from the edge of the fabric. Pull the thread to gather the fabric around the paper circle. Press; remove paper.

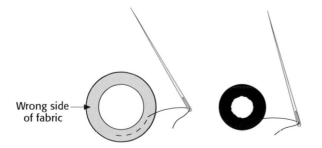

Wrong side of fabric

Appliqué the berry to the background square using the marked lines as a guide for placement. Repeat for remaining berries.

Quilt Assembly

1. Sew 2 appliquéd blocks together using ¼" seam allowances. Press the seam allowances open (this creates equal shadows on both sides of the seam). Repeat for the remaining 2 blocks.

2. Sew the pairs of appliquéd blocks together to make a square. Press the seams open.

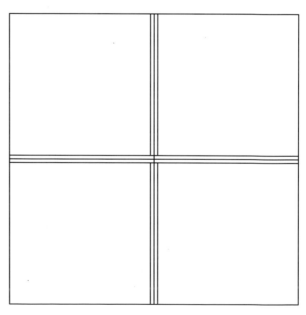

Press seams open.

3. Referring to "Straight-Cut Borders" on page 12, measure, trim, and sew the border strips to the side edges of the quilt top first, and then to the top and bottom edges.

Prairie Points

1. Make 92 Prairie Points by folding 3" squares in half diagonally and in half again to form triangles.

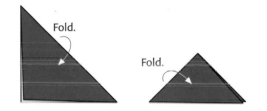

2. Position 1 Prairie Point at the center of one side of the quilt and 1 Prairie Point at each corner on the same side of the quilt, right sides together and raw edges matching. Position the Prairie Points so the open fold of each point faces the same direction.

3. Position 10 Prairie Points between the center and corner points for a total of 23 Prairie Points along one side. Slide the folded edge of one Prairie Point into the open fold of the adjacent point. Pin the points along the edge. Sew the points to the quilt top ¼" from the raw edges.

4. Add Prairie Points to the remaining 3 edges of the quilt top. Butt points at the corners.

5. Fold the Prairie Points out, with points facing away from the center of the quilt; press.

Finishing

1. With the quilt assembled, mark the quilting lines for the wreath border on the quilt, using the pattern created in step 1 on page 17. Mark a diagonal quilting line through the center of the quilt from corner to corner; repeat in the opposite direction. Mark parallel diagonal lines 1" apart across the "background" of the quilt and through the centers of the wreaths.

2. Layer the quilt top, batting, and backing; then baste.

3. Referring to "Quilting Techniques" on page 14, quilt around the edges of the stems, holly leaves, and berries. Quilt the design around the wreath. Quilt the 1" grid in the "background" and in the center of the wreaths. Outline quilt next to the red border.

4. On the back of the quilt, trim the batting to the edge of the quilt top. Trim the backing ¼" larger than the quilt top.

5. Turn the backing under ¼" and hand sew it to the Prairie Points. Add a label to the quilt.

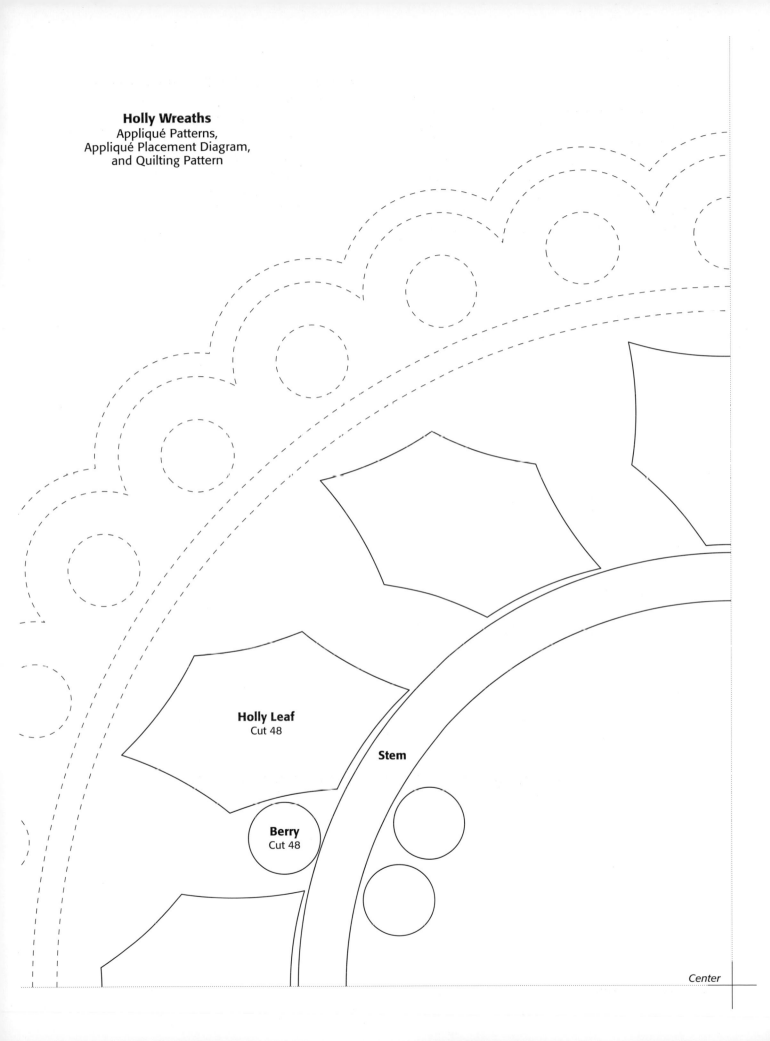

Holly Wreaths
Appliqué Patterns,
Appliqué Placement Diagram,
and Quilting Pattern

Holly Leaf
Cut 48

Stem

Berry
Cut 48

Center

Poinsettia Blossom

Poinsettia Blossom by Amy Whalen Helmkamp, 2000, Lake Oswego, Oregon, 17½" x 19½".

Amy chose to include the poinsettia and candle in her design because to her, they represent the true meaning of the season—God's gift of light and life.

Materials: *42"-wide fabric*

5" x 20" piece mottled dark green for border strips and corner squares

11" x 15" piece mottled pale yellow for wall pieces 1–8

7" x 15" piece mottled brown for table piece 9

3½" x 7½" piece mottled blue for candle piece 10

1½" x 3" piece mottled pale blue for candle top piece 11

2½" x 3½" piece mottled yellow-orange for candle flame piece 12

7" x 8" piece mottled yellow for candle's glow piece 13

2½" square mottled yellow for flower center piece 14

7" x 8½" piece gold-flecked mottled red for top flower petals pieces 15–20

4" x 8" piece mottled dark red for bottom flower petal pieces 21–26

1 yd. black for foundation, backing, binding, and hanging sleeve

20½" x 22½" piece of batting

1½ yd. fusible web

Black cotton thread

.004 monofilament thread (if you use lightweight fusible web that needs to be stitched down)

Cutting

From the black fabric, cut:

2 pieces, 20½" x 22½", for the foundation and backing

2 strips, 2½" x 42", for binding

Preparing the Appliqués

Note: The pattern is the mirror image of your finished quilt. Should you wish to have the finished design face the same direction as the pattern, turn the pattern over and trace the pieces from the back of the pattern.

1. Draw the border pieces onto the fusible web. Using a ruler, draw 2 strips 1" x 13", 2 strips 1" x 15", and 1 square 3" x 3". Draw lines vertically and horizontally through the center of the 3" square, dividing it into 4 equal 1½" squares. The 1" x 15" strips will be the side border strips, the 1" x 13" strips will be the top and bottom border strips, and the 1½" squares will be the corner squares.

2. Trace the pattern sections on pages 26–29 and tape them together to make a full-size pattern. From the quilt pattern, trace the individual pattern pieces onto the paper backing side of the fusible web with a pencil or permanent marking pen. Trace the pattern pieces in groups—all wall pieces together, all top flower petals together, and so on—so that you can press them to their corresponding fabrics without cutting all the small pieces apart. Be sure to copy the pattern number onto your fusible web.

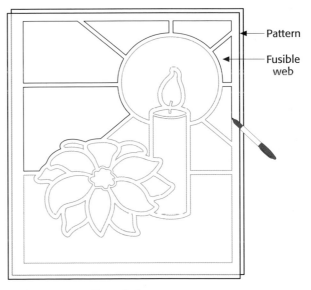

Trace design.

3. After you trace all the pieces, cut the groups apart and fuse them to the wrong side of the appliqué fabrics; refer to the manufacturer's instructions for using the fusible web. Cut out each shape and set the appliqués aside.

Quilt Assembly

1. Using a ruler and a marking pencil, measure in 2" from each edge of the foundation fabric and draw a line the full length of each side to use as guidelines. Draw a second line 2¼" from each edge of the foundation fabric and a third line 3¾" from each edge.

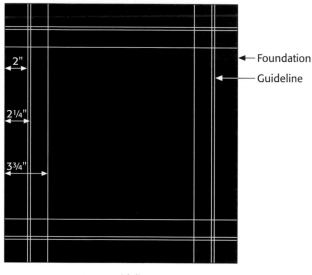

Draw guidelines.

2. Referring to the appliqué guide (right) and the traced pattern, place the corner squares onto the foundation fabric. Lay the outer edge of each square on the outer drawn lines. Next, place the top and bottom border strips on the foundation, laying the edges of the strips on the lines drawn 2¼" and 3¾" from the edges. Leave a ¼" gap between the ends of these strips and the corner squares. You may use a ruler to check your spacing, if you desire. Position the side border strips on the foundation in the same manner.

Appliqué Guide

3. Continuing to work from the outside edges toward the quilt center, place the outside edges of the wall and table pieces on the inner guidelines of the foundation, leaving a ½" gap between them and the border strips. Place the remaining pieces on the foundation. Leave a ¼" gap between all pieces except the flower center; leave an ⅛" gap between the flower center and the surrounding petals.

4. Once you have all of the pieces in place, stand back and study your top. Make any necessary adjustments. Following the manufacturer's directions for your fusible web, press all of the pieces to adhere them to the foundation. Allow the quilt top to cool.

Finishing

1. Layer the quilt top, batting, and backing together; then baste.

2. If you used no-sew fusible web for your appliqués, use black thread and a straight stitch to quilt around your appliqué pieces. Don't stitch through the appliqués; the heavy-duty layer of fusible web may gum up your needle after just a few stitches. If you used a lightweight fusible web for your appliqués, use one of the following stitches to secure your appliqué pieces:

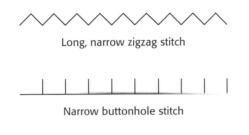

Long, narrow zigzag stitch

Narrow buttonhole stitch

Blind hem stitch

With invisible monofilament thread on top and black thread in the bobbin, stitch around each appliqué piece. You will be sewing down the edges of the appliqué pieces and quilting your quilt at the same time.

Note: You may need to adjust the tension on your sewing machine to accommodate the monofilament thread. It is very lightweight, and you won't want the bobbin thread pulling up to the top of your quilt. Test sew on fabric scraps to see if you will need to tighten or loosen your upper tension.

3. Using a rotary cutter and ruler, trim the quilt top, batting, and backing to ½" from the outside edges of the border pieces.

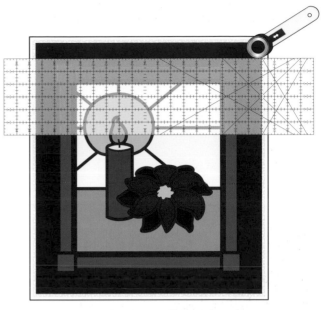

Trim, leaving ½" all around
the outside edges of the border pieces.

4. Bind the edges of your quilt with 2½" binding strips (see "Binding" on page 15). Add a label to your quilt.

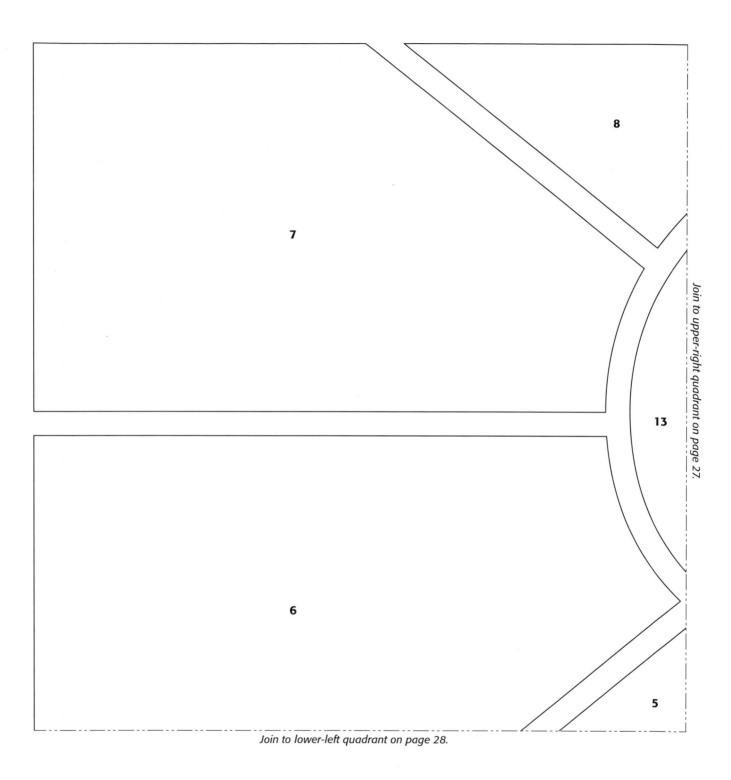

8

7

13

Join to upper-right quadrant on page 27.

6

5

Join to lower-left quadrant on page 28.

Poinsettia Blossom
Upper-Left Quadrant

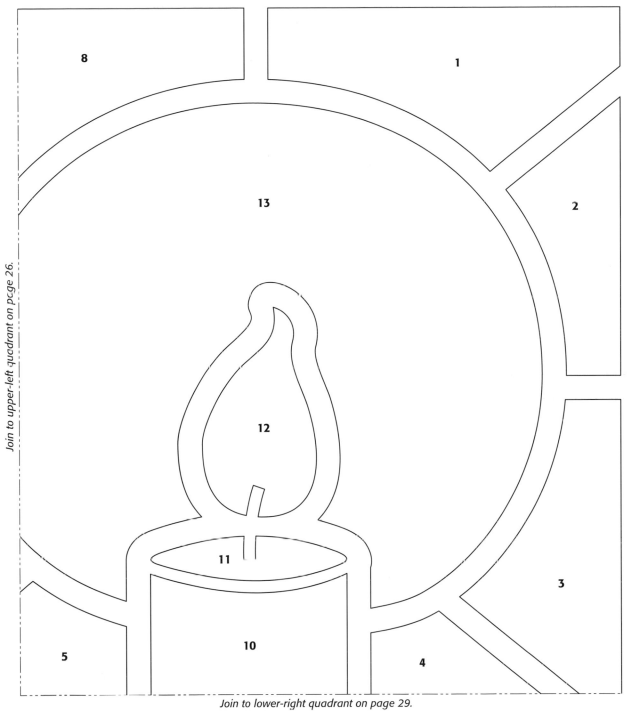

Join to upper-left quadrant on pcge 26.

Join to lower-right quadrant on page 29.

Poinsettia Blossom
Upper-Right Quadrant

Join to upper-left quadrant on page 26.

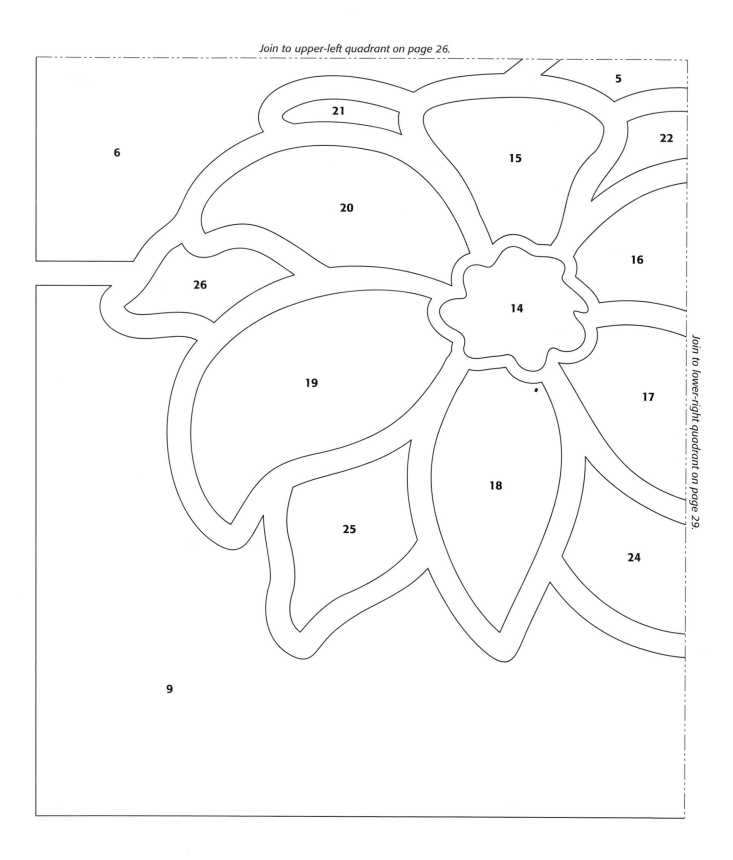

Join to lower-right quadrant on page 29.

Poinsettia Blossom
Lower-Left Quadrant

Join to upper-right quadrant on page 27.

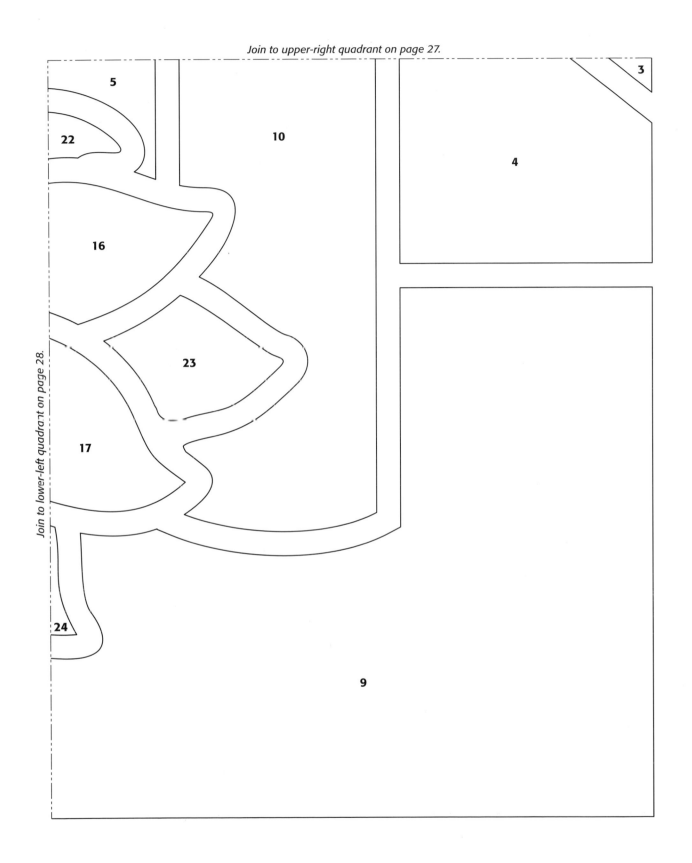

Join to lower-left quadrant on page 28.

Poinsettia Blossom
Lower-Right Quadrant

Deck the Halls

Deck the Halls by Pamela Mostek, 2000, Cheney, Washington, 46" x 46".

You'll be ready for the festive season with this quick-and-easy-to-make scrappy quilt that's just right for your kitchen table or for displaying on a wall. Use all your favorite Christmas red prints. The more the merrier!

Finished Block Size: 8" x 8"

Materials: *42"-wide fabric*

1⅞ yds. total assorted red prints for blocks

1⅝ yds. total assorted tan and white prints for blocks

½ yd. green for leaves

⅛ yd. or scraps of red for berries

⅛ yd. each of 3 red prints for border

¼ yd. of fourth red print for border

2⅞ yd. for backing

½ yd. total assorted red prints for binding

1½ yd. lightweight fusible web

50" x 50" piece of batting

Cutting

From the assorted red prints, cut:

    50 squares, 6½" x 6½", for blocks

From the assorted tan and white prints, cut:

    25 squares, 8½" x 8½", for blocks

From the 3 red border prints, cut:

    3 strips, 3½" x 42", for the bottom and 2 side borders

From the fourth red border print, cut:

    2 strips, 3½" x 42", for the top border

From the assorted red prints for binding, cut:

    Strips, 2¾" wide and assorted lengths, to total approximately 190"

Block Assembly

1. Using a ruler and soft-lead pencil, draw a diagonal line from corner to corner on the back of the red 6½" squares.

2. With right sides together, position one 6½" red square on top of each 8½" tan square, matching upper-left corners as shown. Stitch along diagonal line. Trim ¼" from the stitching line as shown; press seam allowances toward red fabric.

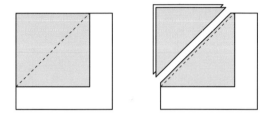

3. Position a red square on the bottom right hand corner of each tan square, right sides together. Stitch along diagonal line. Trim ¼" from the stitching line as before and press seam allowances toward red fabric to complete block.

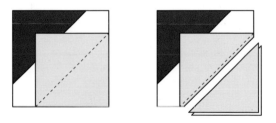

Make 25.

4. Select 13 of the blocks for holly appliqués and set aside the remaining 12 blocks.

5. Referring to "Fusible Appliqué" on page 10 and the appliqué patterns on page 33, make 26 leaf and 13 berry appliqués. Fuse 2 leaves each to 13 blocks, overlapping slightly as shown. Fuse 1 berry to the tips of each pair of holly leaves.

Make 13.

6. Using black or dark thread, machine or hand buttonhole stitch around all edges of the holly leaves and berries (see "Buttonhole Stitch" on page 11).

Quilt Assembly

1. Arrange the blocks in 5 rows of 5 blocks each, alternating appliquéd blocks and nonappliquéd blocks. Sew the blocks into horizontal rows. Join the rows. Press.

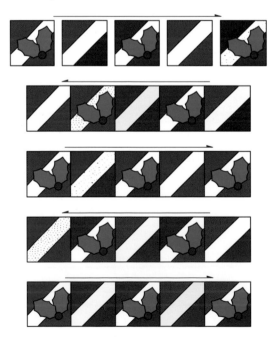

2. Measure the width of the quilt top from side to side at the center. From one of the 3 red border fabrics, cut a border strip to this measurement. Sew the border strip to the right edge of the quilt top. Press seam toward border.

3. Measure the width of the quilt top through the center, including the right border just added. From a second red border fabric, cut a border strip to this measurement. Sew the border strip to the bottom edge of the quilt top. Press the seam toward the border.

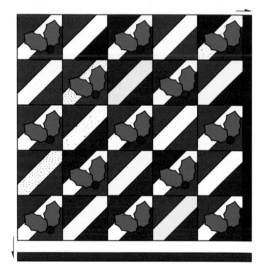

4. Measure the length of the quilt top from top to bottom at the center, including the bottom border just added. From the third red border fabric, cut the left border strip to this measurement. Sew the border strip to the left edge of the quilt. Press the seam toward the border.

5. Measure the width of the quilt top through the center, including the side border strips just added. Sew together the 2 border strips from the fourth red border fabric, and trim to this measurement for the top border strip. Sew the border strip to the top edge of the quilt top. Press the seam toward the border.

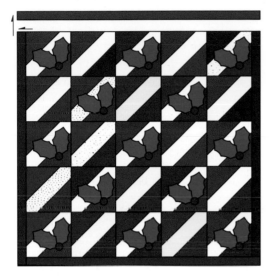

Finishing

1. Layer the quilt top, batting, and backing; then baste.

2. Quilt the entire top, including the appliqués, with a free-motion, all-over design (see "Machine Quilting" on page 14).

3. To make multi-fabric binding, sew together the 2¾" strips from the various red fabrics to make a 190" continuous strip. Bind the quilt (see "Binding" on page 15). Add a label.

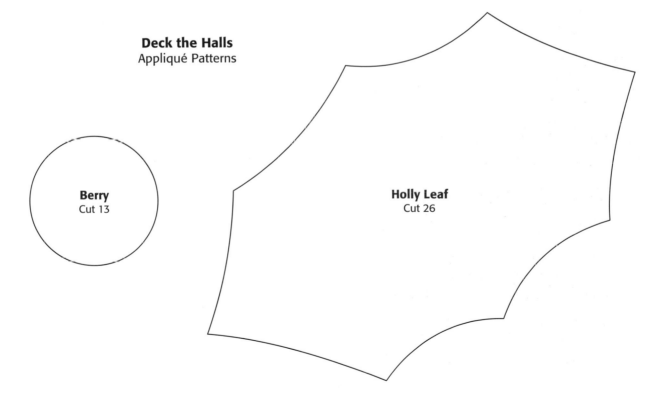

Deck the Halls
Appliqué Patterns

Berry
Cut 13

Holly Leaf
Cut 26

Joyful Tidings

Joyful Tidings by Gretchen Hudock, 2000, Slinger, Wisconsin, 25" x 25".

Gretchen sketched the design for this quilt several years ago and filed it away in hopes of creating it at a future date. This book provided the perfect opportunity! The quilt's small size makes it a quick project to create for holiday gift giving.

Finished Block Size: 6" x 6

Materials: *42"-wide fabric*

¼ yd. red for blocks

½ yd. tan print for background

¼ yd. red plaid for blocks and inner border

¼ yd. green for blocks and inner border

⅜ yd. green print for center block and outer border

¼ yd. for binding

⅞ yd. for backing

29" x 29" piece of batting

Cutting

From the tan print, cut:

3 strips, 3½" x 42"; crosscut the strips into:

20 rectangles, 2" x 3½", for background

8 squares, 3½" x 3½", for background

4 rectangles, 3½" x 6½", for background

2 squares, 3⅞" x 3⅞"; cut squares once diagonally to make 4 triangles for background

8 squares, 2" x 2", for background

From the red fabric, cut:

2 strips, 2" x 42"; crosscut into 24 squares, each 2" x 2", for blocks

From the red plaid, cut:

1 square, 3½" x 3½", for center block

2 squares, 3⅞" x 3⅞", for corner blocks

2 squares, 1⅞" x 1⅞", for inner border

From the green fabric, cut:

2 squares, 3⅞" x 3⅞", for blocks

4 squares, 2⅜" x 2⅜"; cut squares once diagonally to make 8 triangles for blocks

2 squares, 1⅞" x 1⅞", for inner border

2 strips, 1½" x 42"; crosscut into 4 strips, each 1½" x 18½", for inner border

From the green print, cut:

4 rectangles, 3½" x 6½", for center block

2 strips, 2½" x 20½", for outer border

2 strips, 2½" x 24½", for outer border

From the fabric for the binding, cut:

3 strips, 2" x 42"

Quilt Assembly

1. Using a ruler and soft-leaded pencil, draw a diagonal line from corner to corner on the back of the red 2" squares.

2. Position one 2" red square on top of a 2" x 3½" tan rectangle, right sides together, matching left edges as shown. Stitch along diagonal line. Trim ¼" from the stitching line; press seam toward red fabric. Stitch a red square to the right side of the rectangle in the same manner to make star points.

Make 12.

3. Join 4 star-point units, four 2" tan squares, and one 3½" plaid square to make 1 center Star Block.

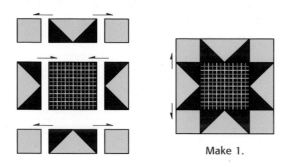

Make 1.

4. Using a ruler and soft-leaded pencil, draw a diagonal line from corner to corner on the back of the red plaid 3⅞" squares. Place plaid squares over green 3⅞" squares, right sides together. Sew scant ¼" seam on each side of diagonal line. Press flat. Cut along diagonal. Press seams open to make four 3½" bias squares.

5. Sew green triangles to remaining tan 2" x 3½" rectangles as shown to make 4 left-side units and 4 right-side units for each corner block.

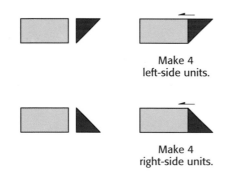

Make 4
left-side units.

Make 4
right-side units.

6. Join 2 star-point units, one 2" tan square, a green and red-plaid bias square, 1 right-side unit, 1 left-side unit, and a tan triangle to make 1 corner block.

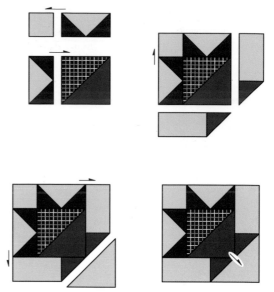

Make 4
corner blocks.

7. Using a ruler and soft-leaded pencil, draw a diagonal line from corner to corner on the back of the tan 3½" squares.

8. Position one 3½" tan square on top of a 3½" x 6½" green print rectangle, right sides together, matching left edges. Stitch along diagonal line. Trim ¼" from the stitching line; press seam toward tan fabric. Stitch a tan square to the right side of the rectangle in the same manner to make 1 pieced unit. Repeat to make 4 units.

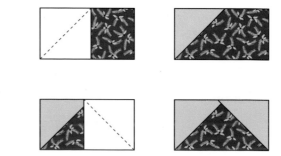

Make 4.

9. Join 1 unit from step 8 to one 3½" x 6½" tan rectangle as shown.

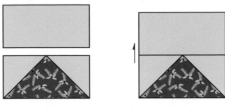

Make 4.

10. Join 4 corner blocks, 4 units assembled in step 9, and 1 center block.

11. Using a ruler and soft-leaded pencil, draw a diagonal line from corner to corner on the back of the red-plaid 1⅞" squares. Place plaid squares over green 1⅞" squares, right sides together. Sew a scant ¼" seam on each side of diagonal line. Press flat. Cut along diagonal. Press seams open to make 4 bias squares. Set aside.

12. Referring to "Borders with Corner Squares" on page 12, measure, trim, and sew the inner-border strips to the side edges of the quilt top first. Then sew the inner-border strips to the top and bottom edges, using the bias squares from step 11 for the corner squares.

13. Referring to "Straight-Cut Borders" on page 12, measure, trim, and sew the outer-border strips to the side edges of the quilt top first, and then to the top and bottom edges.

Finishing

1. Layer the quilt top, batting, and backing; then baste. Quilt as desired.

2. Bind the edges of the quilt and add a label.

Christmas Argyle

Christmas Argyle by Judy Pollard, 2000, Seattle, Washington, 59" x 79".
Machine quilted by Frankie Schmitt.

The red, white, and gold colors in this quilt call to mind the glitter and gaiety of the season.
The floral border and sashing fabric make it a quilt that can be enjoyed year round.

Finished Block Size: 6" x 6"

Materials: *42"-wide fabric*

1⅛ yds. dark red print for blocks and setting squares

½ yd. red plaid for blocks

½ yd. red print #1

⅜ yd. red print #2

1 yd. yellow print for blocks

1 yd. white print for blocks

2¾ yds. floral print for sashing and border

⅝ yd. for binding

3¾ yds. for backing

63" x 83" piece of batting

Cutting

From dark red print, cut:

63 squares, 3½" x 3½", for blocks

4 squares, 5½" x 5½"; cut squares twice diagonally to make 16 triangles for half blocks and corner blocks (only 14 triangles will be used)

58 squares, 1½" x 1½", for setting squares

6 squares 2¾" x 2¾"; cut squares twice diagonally to make 24 triangles for setting half squares.

From the red plaid, cut:

25 squares, 3½" x 3½", for blocks

2 squares, 5½" x 5½"; cut squares twice diagonally to make 8 triangles for half blocks and corner blocks (only 5 will be needed)

From red print #1, cut:

19 squares, 3½" x 3½", for blocks

1 square, 5½" x 5½"; cut square twice diagonally to make 4 triangles for half blocks

From red print #2, cut:

15 squares, 3½" x 3½", for blocks

3 squares, 5½" x 5½"; cut squares twice diagonally to make 12 triangles for half blocks and corner blocks (only 9 will be needed)

From yellow print, cut:

65 squares, 3½" x 3½", for blocks

3 squares 5½" x 5½"; cut squares twice diagonally to make 12 triangles for blocks and corner blocks (only 10 will be needed)

From the white print, cut:

65 squares, 3½" x 3½", for blocks

3 squares 5½" x 5½"; cut squares twice diagonally to make 12 triangles for blocks and corner blocks (only 10 will be needed)

From the floral print, cut:

2 strips, 72" x 4¾", for side border strips

2 strips, 61" x 4¾", for top and bottom border strips

140 strips, 6½" x 1½", for sashing

From the fabric for the binding, cut:

7 strips, 2" x 42"

Block Assembly

1. Join 1 red print or plaid square, 1 dark red-print square, 1 white square, and 1 yellow square to make a Four Patch block as shown below (Block A).

Make 14 with red plaid. Make 11 with red print #1. Make 10 with red print #2.

2. Join 1 red print or plaid square, 1 dark red-print square, 1 white square, and 1 yellow square to make a Four Patch block as shown below (Block B—the positions of white square and yellow square are reversed from Block A).

Make 11 with red plaid. Make 8 with red print #1. Make 5 with red print #2.

3. Join 1 dark red-print square, 1 yellow triangle, and 1 white triangle to make Half Block A (shown below).

Make 4.

4. Join 1 red print or plaid square, 1 yellow triangle, and 1 white triangle to make Half Block B as shown below (positions of white triangle and yellow triangle are reversed from Half Block A).

Make 1 with red plaid. Make 2 with red print #1. Make 1 with red print #2.

5. Join 1 yellow square, 1 dark red-print triangle, and 1 red-print or plaid triangle to make Half Block C as shown below.

Make 2 with red plaid. Make 1 with red print #1. Make 3 with red print #2.

6. Join 1 white square, 1 dark red-print triangle, and 1 red-print or plaid triangle to make Half Block D as shown below.

Make 1 with red plaid. Make 1 with red print #1. Make 4 with red print #2.

7. Join 4 red triangles, 2 white triangles, and 2 yellow triangles to make the 4 corner blocks shown below.

Corner blocks
Make 1 each.

Quilt Assembly and Finishing

1. Arrange the blocks into diagonal rows alternating A blocks and B blocks. Begin and end rows of blocks at sides of quilt with Half Blocks A, B, C, and D. Use the photo on page 38 as a guide for arranging the blocks into an argyle pattern. Between rows of blocks, join rows of sashing and setting squares, beginning and ending each row with a setting half square. Add a corner block to each corner of the quilt.

2. Referring to "Straight-Cut Borders" on page 12, measure, trim, and sew the border strips to the side edges of the quilt top first, and then to the top and bottom edges.

3. Layer the quilt top, batting, and backing; then baste. Quilt as desired.

4. Bind the edges of the quilt and add a label.

Christmas Snowguy

Christmas Snowguy by Vicki Garnas, 2000, Granada Hills, California, 22½" x 24½".

The stenciled snowman has a red-and-green felt appliquéd jacket to keep him warm. In different colors, he can be a cozy addition to your home all winter long.

Materials: *42"-wide fabric*

10½" x 13" piece of muslin for background

8" x 12" piece of red felt for coat, pockets, and ear muffs

5" x 6" piece of green felt for collar, cuffs, and tree trims

¼ yd. red plaid for inner border

¾ yd. green print #1 for outer border and binding

¾ yd. for backing

2½" x 15" piece of green print for tree

2" x 42" piece of torn red fabric for bow

24" x 24½" piece of cotton batting

Freezer paper for stencils

Small scissors

Iron

Black embroidery floss

Acrylic craft paint in white, brown, red, and orange

Paper plate

Cosmetic sponge wedges

Paper towels

Black Sharpie markers in fine and ultra-fine sizes

Gray permanent marker

Red pencil

Embroidery floss to match appliqués

Embroidery needle

Small wooden birdhouse

Emery board or fine sandpaper

Small twig for birdhouse roof

Fabric glue

1¼" twig or toothpick for nose

Pinking shears

9" stick for tree

5 small pinecones

2 miniature cardinal birds

7 buttons in different sizes and colors

3 white ½" buttons

9 beads

1 bell

Cutting

From red plaid fabric, cut:

3 strips, 1¾" x 42", for inner border

From green print #1, cut:

3 strips, 4½" x 42", for outer border

3 strips, 2" x 42", for binding

Stenciling

1. Trace the snowman stencil patterns (pages 47–48) onto freezer paper. Cut out and remove the head and body pieces from stencil 1 and the earmuff band and arm pieces from stencil 2.

2. Center stencil 1 on top of muslin background, shiny side down; fuse stencil to fabric with a dry iron set for cotton.

3. Cover work area with a piece of freezer paper. Pour a small amount of white paint onto a paper plate. Grasp a dry cosmetic sponge on opposite sides with your thumb and index finger. The exposed area at the bottom of the sponge will be your painting surface.

Cosmetic sponge
wedge

4. Dip the cosmetic sponge into the white paint. Blot on a paper towel several times to remove excess paint. Apply paint to fabric in the head and body openings on the stencil, painting around the edge of the stencil in an up-and-down motion or a round-and-round motion. Gradually work paint toward the center of the stencil opening with the same motion until the area is covered. Apply a second coat of paint if necessary for coverage.

5. Align stencil 2 over the painted head and body; fuse in place. Stencil earmuff band and twig arms brown.

6. Following the "Pen-work details" on page 46, outline the snowman body and head with the fine Sharpie marker. Outline the twig arms and the earmuff band. Draw in a smile, the eyes, and the eyebrows. Scribble just inside the body outline with the ultra-fine Sharpie marker. Draw in the ground line below the snowman's body. Shade the edges of the white painted areas with the gray marker. Draw rosy cheeks on the snowman using the red pencil. Heat set the paints by ironing with a hot iron.

Appliqué

1. Trace the patterns for the coat, left and right collar, left and right muff, and left and right pockets onto freezer paper and cut out. Iron the patterns to the right side of the corresponding felt pieces. Cut out the patterns, cutting slightly outside the edges of the paper. (The felt seems to shrink a bit during the appliqué process, so cutting the pieces a bit larger is helpful.) Remove the freezer paper.

2. With matching thread, appliqué the coat to the stenciled snowman. Use a small running stitch at the edge of the felt.

3. Appliqué the collar, cuffs, and pockets in the same manner. Then tack the tree trims to the pockets and tack the earmuffs in place. Outline the armholes with black embroidery floss. Refer to "Outline Stitch" on page 45 and the pattern on page 49. Use a running stitch to divide the coat at the center front.

4. Trim the stenciled muslin block to even edges.

Assembly and Finishing

1. Sew each inner border strip to an outer border strip, right sides together, along one long edge.

2. Referring to "Straight-Cut Borders" on page 12, measure, trim, and sew the border strips to the side edges of the quilt top first, and then to the top and bottom edges.

3. Layer the quilt top, batting, and backing; then baste. Quilt around the edges of the border strips and around the snowman figure.

4. Bind the edges of the quilt and add a label.

5. Tie the torn red fabric strip into a large looped bow with very long loops. With 3 strands of embroidery floss, sew the knot of the bow to the center of the quilt's top border. Fold out the bow loops. Hand gather along the length of the loops; tack in place.

6. Paint the small wooden birdhouse red and paint the roof white. Dab brown paint on top of the red and white, and then wipe it away with a cloth. Use an emery board or sandpaper to remove some paint and roughen the edges of the birdhouse. Tie a length of embroidery floss to a twig cut slightly longer than the birdhouse roof. Glue the twig to the top of the birdhouse.

7. Paint a small twig orange for the nose; add white paint to the top for snow. Allow to dry, and then glue to snowman.

8. Fold green 2½" x 15" strip of fabric in half lengthwise; press. On unfolded edge, with pinking shears, cut fringe about ¼" wide along length of fabric; do not cut through the fold. Dab glue onto half of the 9" stick. Wrap the fringed fabric around the stick to the top, overlap the top, and continue back down the stick, securing with glue. Fluff the fringe up for the tree; set aside to dry. Paint small pine cones white and glue them to the tree. Glue 1 miniature cardinal to the tree. Sew the tree to the snowman's arm and tack the treetop to quilt top.

9. Arrange assorted buttons in a cluster on top of the bow at the center. Sew buttons on with 3-strand embroidery floss going all the way through the quilt. Sew the white ½" buttons to the coat front.

10. Sew the birdhouse to the snowman's hand with embroidery floss. Thread 9 beads and a bell on 3 strands of floss, ending with the bell. Rethread the embroidery floss through the beads to the top and sew down to the snowman's hand. Glue the remaining miniature cardinal to the snowman's hand.

Outline Stitch

Pull the needle through the fabric at point A, insert at point B, and exit at point C, keeping the thread to the left of the needle. Repeat.

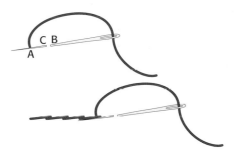

Pen-work details

Christmas Snowguy
Stencil 1

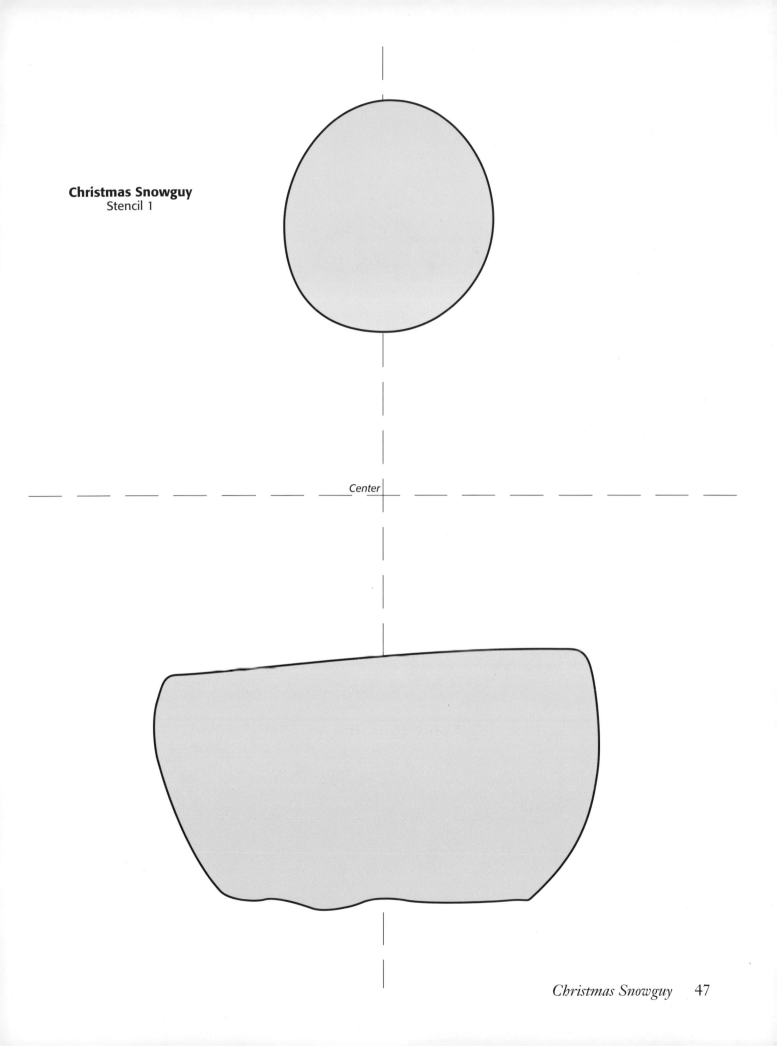

Center

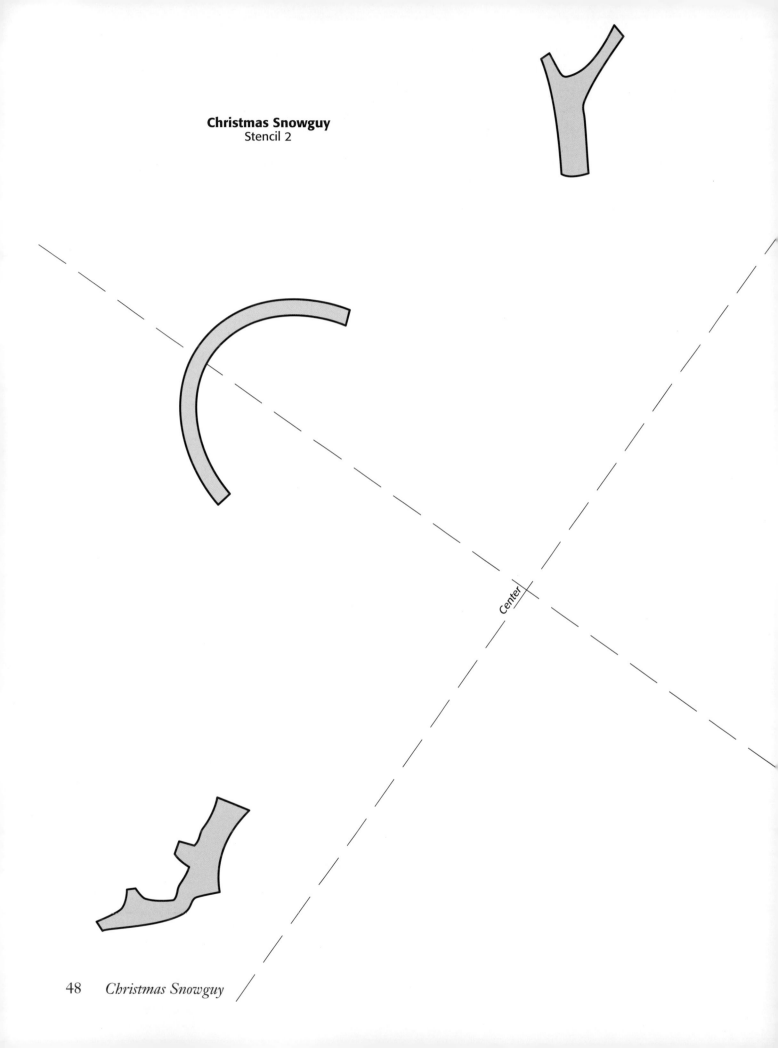

Christmas Snowguy
Stencil 2

Center

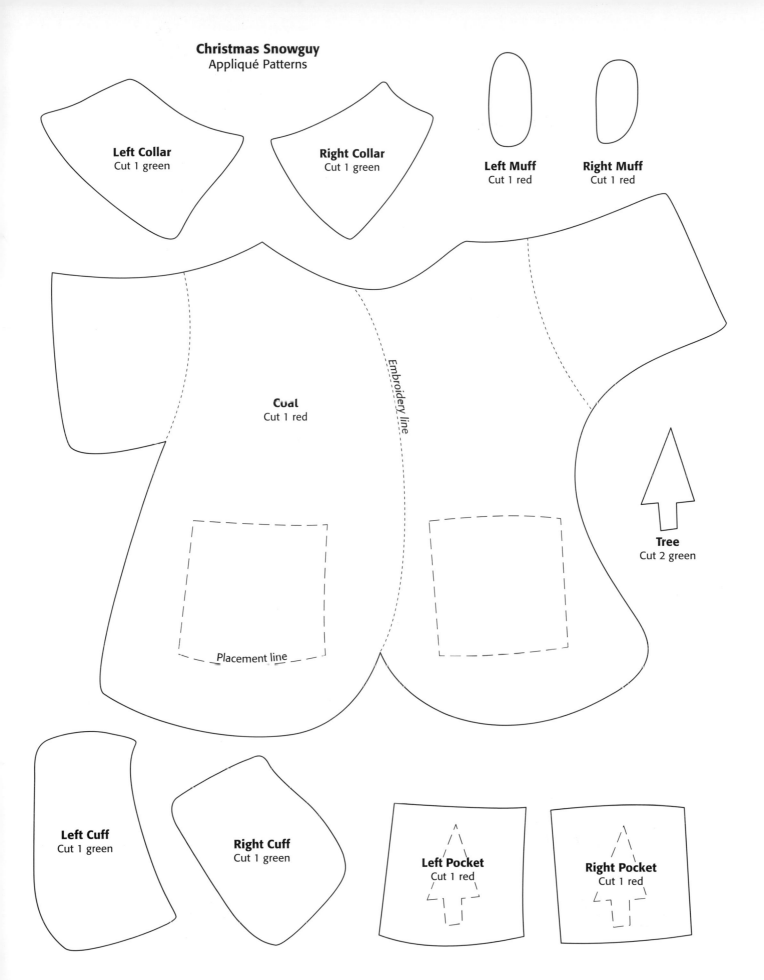

Christmas Snowguy
Appliqué Patterns

Left Collar
Cut 1 green

Right Collar
Cut 1 green

Left Muff
Cut 1 red

Right Muff
Cut 1 red

Coal
Cut 1 red

Embroidery line

Tree
Cut 2 green

Placement line

Left Cuff
Cut 1 green

Right Cuff
Cut 1 green

Left Pocket
Cut 1 red

Right Pocket
Cut 1 red

Winter Solstice by Jean Van Bockel, 2000, Coeur d'Alene, Idaho, 26" x 26".

A colorful December sunset inspired "Winter Solstice." Sewn in nontraditional Christmas fabrics, this quilt can grace your home until the crocuses appear.

Materials: *42"-wide fabric*

1 fat quarter blue or blue print for sky

1 fat quarter white for snow

Scraps of green for holly leaves, trees, and shrubs

Scraps of red for holly berries and door

Scrap of yellow for windows

Scrap of brown for house and chimney

Scrap of light gray for roof

Scrap of mottled off-white for smoke

Scrap of mottled light pink for sunset

Scrap of medium gray for path

⅛ yd. gold for border of winter scene

½ yd. teal for setting triangles and sawtooth border

1 fat quarter brown for holly stem

¼ yd. white-on-white print for sawtooth border

⅛ yd. light green for inner border

1 yd. dark green print for outer border, backing, and binding

Brown embroidery floss

⅛" bias bar

½ yd. fusible web (if not hand appliquéing)

28" x 28" piece of batting

Cutting

From blue fabric, cut:

   1 square, 10¼" x 10¼", for sky

From gold fabric, cut:

   2 strips, 1" x 10¼", for border of winter scene

   2 strips, 1" x 11¼", for border of winter scene

From teal fabric, cut:

   2 squares, 8⅜" x 8⅜", for the setting triangles; cut squares once diagonally to make 4 triangles

   12 squares, 3⅜" x 3⅜"; cut squares once diagonally to make 24 triangles for sawtooth border

From brown fat quarter, cut:

   4 bias strips, ¾"x 14", for holly stem

From white fabric, cut:

   12 squares, 3⅜"x 3⅜"; cut squares once diagonally to make 24 triangles for sawtooth border

   4 squares, 3" x 3", for sawtooth border

From light green fabric, cut:

   2 strips 1½" x 20½", for inner border

   2 strips, 1½" x 22½", for inner border

From dark green print fabric, cut:

   1 square, 28" x 28", for backing

   2 strips, 2½" x 22½", for outer border

   2 strips, 2½" x 26½", for outer border

   3 strips, 2" x 42", for binding

Quilt Assembly

Note: See "Basic Appliqué" on page 8 for general information.

1. Trace pattern shapes on pages 54–55 onto paper. For needle-turn appliqué, cut shapes from appropriate fabrics, adding 1/16" seam allowance around all pieces. Transfer design lines for windows and door onto the house piece.

2. Appliqué the pattern pieces to the sky square using the numbered order on the pattern as a guide. Follow the instructions for needle-turn appliqué on page 9. Use reverse appliqué (page 9) for pieces 1, 8, 9, and 10.

3. Outline the windows, door, and corner line of house with three strands of embroidery floss using an outline stitch (page 45), if desired.

4. Sew the two 1" x 10¼" gold border strips to opposite sides of the appliquéd square; press. Sew the 1" x 11¼" gold strips to the remaining sides; press.

5. Sew the teal setting triangles to opposite sides of the unit; press. Sew the remaining setting triangles to the remaining sides; press.

6. Fold a ¾" x 14" brown bias strip lenthwise, wrong sides together. Stitch down the center of the strip; trim raw edges 1/8" from stitching. Insert 1/8" bias bar into tube. Press tube flat, pressing seam allowances to back side. Cut a 3½" piece from one end of the tube to use for one of the holly branches. Repeat with remaining 3 bias strips.

7. Open seam in gold borders ¼" at desired locations for holly stems; insert stems and stitch closed. Pin stems in place. Referring to the photo on page 50, determine desired locations for holly branches on the holly stems. Tuck 3½" branch pieces under stems at desired locations; pin in place. Appliqué stems and branches in place with the traditional appliqué stitch (page 8).

8. Sew each white triangle to a teal triangle along the long diagonal edge to make bias squares. Press toward the teal triangle.

Make 24.

9. Arrange and sew 6 bias squares from step 8 into a strip set as shown. Make 4.

Make 4.

10. Sew a white 3" square to each end of 2 strip sets.

Make 2.

11. Sew the 2 short strip sets to the side edges of the appliquéd square; press seams toward the border. Sew the strips with end squares to the top and bottom edges of the appliquéd square; press seams toward the border.

12. Trace the holly leaf and berry patterns on page 55 and cut out 32 holly leaves from the 2 holly leaf patterns and 24 holly berries, as for the previous appliqué pieces. Appliqué the pieces to the teal setting triangles, following the instructions for "Needle-Turn Appliqué" on page 9.

13. Referring to "Straight-Cut Borders" on page 12, measure, trim, and sew the inner-border strips to the side edges of the quilt top first, then to the top and bottom edges. Repeat for the outer-border strips.

Finishing

1. Layer the quilt top, batting, and backing; then baste. Quilt as desired.

2. Bind the edges of the quilt and add a label.

Tip: In place of appliqués, you can use buttons or beads for the holly berries, if desired.

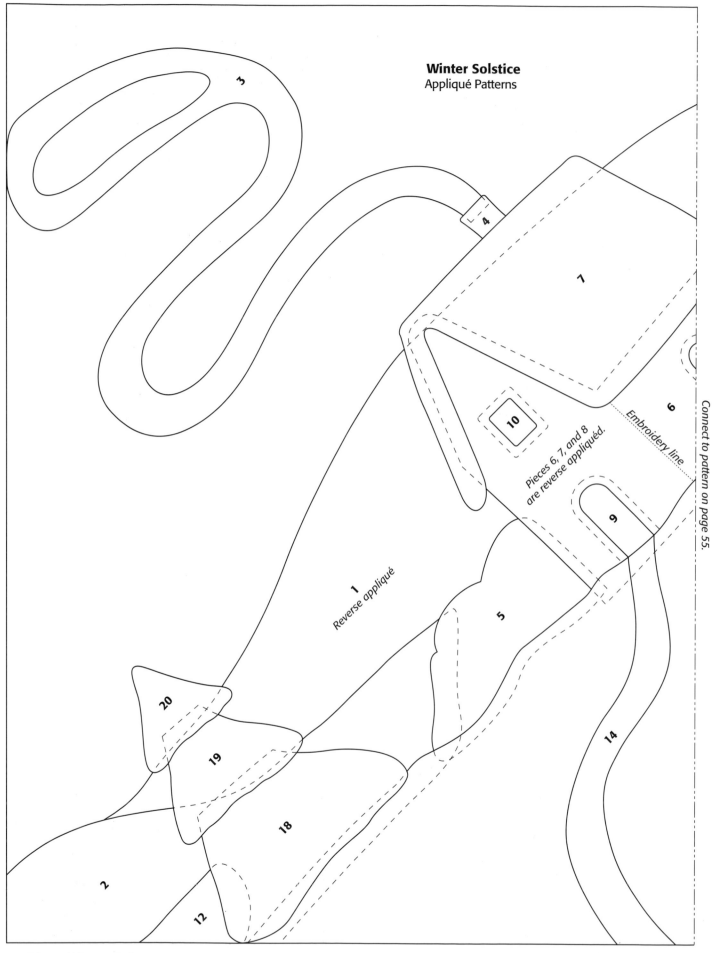

Winter Solstice
Appliqué Patterns

3

4

7

10

*Pieces 6, 7, and 8
are reverse appliquéd.*

6

Embroidery line

Connect to pattern on page 55.

9

1
Reverse appliqué

5

14

20

19

18

2

12

Winter Solstice
Appliqué Patterns

Holly Berry
Cut 24

Holly Leaf
Cut 16

Holly Leaf
Cut 16

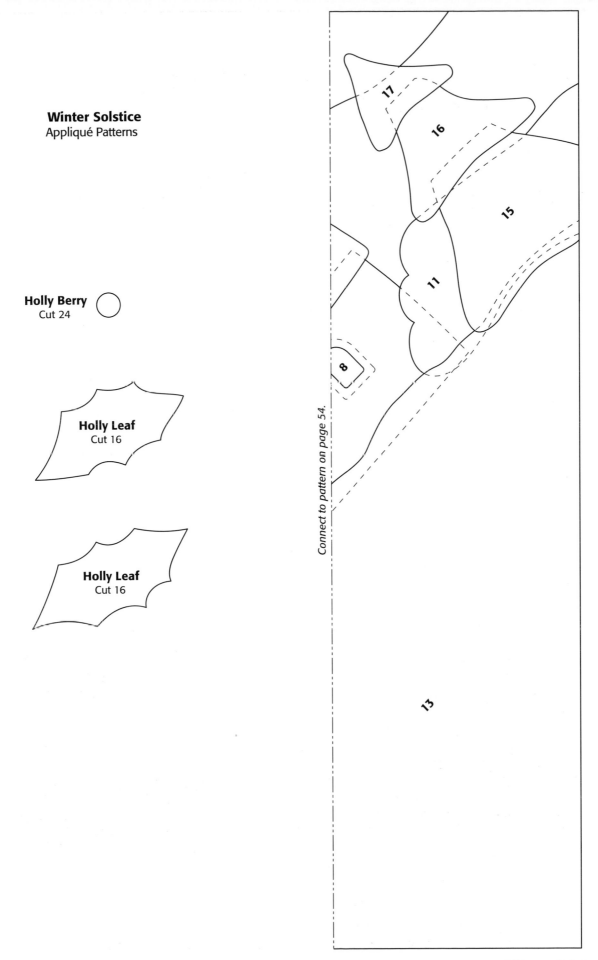

17

16

15

11

8

Connect to pattern on page 54.

13

Christmas Tulips

Christmas Tulips by Tricia Lund, 2000, Seattle, Washington, 40" x 52¼".
Machine quilted by Eileen Merrick.

During the shortest days of the year, this quilt brightens the spirit with its happy
reminder of spring. Although it looks complex, foundation piecing makes it easy.

Finished Block Size: 7" x 7"
Finished Setting Block Size: 3½" x 3½"

Materials: *42"-wide fabric*

1¼ yds. assorted red prints for flower petals, flower centers, and border

1 yd. assorted green prints for stems and leaves

2⅝ yds. assorted ivory and light beige prints for background

1 yd. navy print for sashing and corner blocks

44" x 57" piece of batting

1¾ yds. for backing

½ yd. for binding

Cutting

From the assorted red prints, cut:

A total of 6 strips, 1¾" x 42", for block flower petals and flower centers

A total of 7 strips, 1¼" x 42", for setting block flower petals and flower centers

4"-wide strips (cut on lengthwise grain), for pieced outer border. You will need at least 164" total.

From the assorted green prints, cut:

A total of 5 strips, ¾" x 42", for stems for blocks and setting blocks

A total of 12 strips, 1½" x 42", for leaves for blocks and setting blocks

From the assorted ivory and beige prints, cut:

A total of 10 strips, 1¾" x 42", for flower block background

A total of 7 strips, 3½" x 42", for flower block background

A total of 12 strips, 1¼" x 42", for setting block background

A total of 8 strips, 2" x 42", for setting block background

From the navy print, cut:

4 strips, 7½" x 42"; crosscut the strips into 31 strips, 4" x 7½", for sashing

4 squares, 4" x 4", for corner blocks

From the binding fabric, cut:

6 strips, 2" x 42"

General Foundation Piecing Guidelines

1. The unit that you place under the presser foot consists of 3 layers: the paper foundation (with the marked side up) on top and 2 layers of fabric, right sides together, beneath the paper.

2. Use 12–15 stitches per inch to anchor the stitches well. Backstitch at the ends of sewing lines. If you make a mistake and have to take out a seam, put a piece of tape over the perforated seam on the marked side of the paper.

3. The sewing sequence is numbered on the foundation. Be sure to rotate the foundation so that the numbers are right side up as you sew the unit.

4. If you are not sure if the next fabric piece will cover its allotted space, place a pin along the sewing line instead of sewing and open the piece to see if it fits. If necessary, adjust and test again. An asterisk on the foundation indicates that you should take extra care to see that the piece will fit.

5. Do not remove the paper foundation until you are ready to sew the units into blocks. This helps prevent the distortion that can be caused by handling.

6. The finished unit is a mirror image of the foundation. For example, the leaf on the left side of the paper foundation will be on the right side of the finished block.

Pattern Preparation

1. Photocopy Flower Unit A, Flower Unit B, and Leaf Unit C on pages 63–64 twelve times for the blocks. Cut each unit apart, leaving ⅛" to ¼" around the cutting line.

2. Photocopy Flower Unit D, Flower Unit E, and Leaf Unit F on page 64 twenty times for the setting block. Cut each unit apart, leaving ⅛" to ¼" around the cutting line.

Block Assembly

Flower Unit A and Flower Unit B

Fabric	Pattern Position
1¾" strip flower center fabric	1
1¾" strip background fabric	2, 3, 6, 7, 8
1¾" strip flower petal fabric	4, 5

1. Place a fabric strip for flower center (position 1) and a background fabric strip right sides together. With the marked side of the pattern up, place the fabrics, flower-center fabric up, under the pattern, beneath position 1, with ¼" seam allowance extending into position 2.

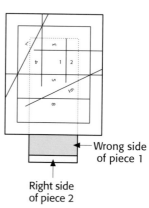

Wrong side of piece 1

Right side of piece 2

2. Hold the fabrics in position and place the unit under the presser foot, paper side up. Sew along the line between positions 1 and 2, through the paper and both layers of fabric.

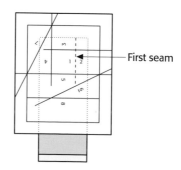

First seam

3. Trim the strips at the end of the stitching line. Fold back piece 2 and press.

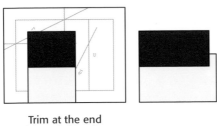

Trim at the end
of the stitching line.

4. Place a strip of background fabric for piece 3 right sides together with fabrics in positions 1 and 2; sew along seam line, trim the seam allowances to ¼", fold piece back, and press.

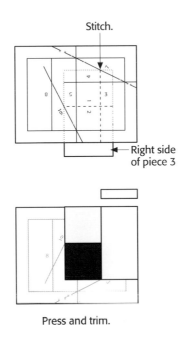

5. Continue to add strips of fabric in order, trimming and pressing after each one. When Flower Unit A is complete, trim along outside cutting line of pattern.

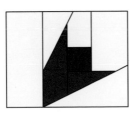

6. Make 12 of Flower Unit A and 12 of Flower Unit B following steps 1 to 5 above.

Leaf Unit C

Fabric	*Pattern Position*
1¾" strip background fabric	1
¾" strip stem fabric	2, 3
3½" strip background fabric	4, 5, 10, 11
1½" strip leaf fabric	6, 7, 8, 9

1. Place background strip and stem strip right sides together, aligning right edge. With the marked side of the paper up, place the fabrics beneath position 1, with the background fabric against the paper and ¼" seam allowance extending into position 2.

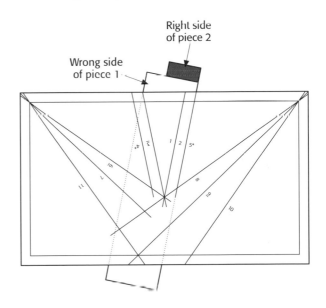

2. Hold the fabrics in position and place the unit under the presser foot, paper side up. Sew along the line between positions 1 and 2, through the paper and both layers of fabric.

First seam

3. Trim the strips at the ends of the stitching line at the bottom. Fold back piece 2 and press. Trim strips at top just outside edge of foundation.

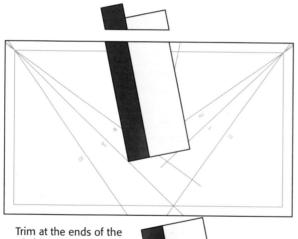

Trim at the ends of the stitching line at bottom and just outside edge of foundation at the top.

4. Place a strip of stem fabric right sides together over background fabric in position 1, with stem fabric extending ¼" into position 3; be sure that the #3 on the paper foundation is right side up. Sew along stitching line between positions 1 and 3. Trim excess stem strip off and trim seam allowances to ¼". Trim remaining stem strip off just outside edge of foundation. Turn and press.

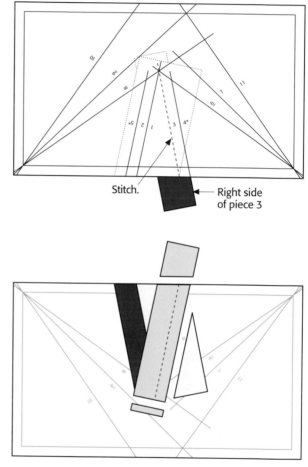

Stitch.

Right side of piece 3

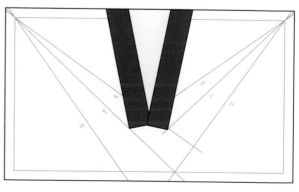

Trim.

Press.

5. Continue to add strips of fabric in order, trimming and pressing after each one. Make sure that the numbers on the foundation are right side up as you sew them. Pay extra attention to the 4 and 5 positions to make sure that the fabric will cover its allotted space when turned and pressed. When Leaf Unit C is complete, trim along outside cutting line.

6. Make 12 of Leaf Unit C following steps 1 to 5 above.

Block Construction

1. Carefully remove paper from Units A, B, and C.

2. Sew Units A and B together. Press seam toward Unit B.

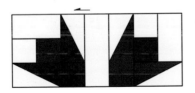

3. Sew Unit C to Unit A-B. Press seam toward Unit A-B.

Setting Block Construction

Flower Unit D and Flower Unit E

Fabric	Pattern Position
1¼" strip flower center fabric	1
1¼" strip background fabric	2, 3, 6, 7, 8
1¼" strip flower petal fabric	4, 5

Note: Scraps from block unit construction can be used instead of strips, if desired.

Using the strips indicated above, make 20 of Flower Unit D and 20 of Flower Unit E, following the instructions for Flower Unit A and Flower Unit B on pages 63–64.

Leaf Unit F

Fabric	Pattern Position
1¼" strip background fabric	1
¾" strip stem fabric	2, 3
2" strip background fabric	4, 5, 8, 9
1½" strip leaf fabric	6, 7

Note: Scraps from block unit construction can be used instead of strips, if desired.

Using the strips indicated above, make 20 of Leaf Unit F, following the instructions for Leaf Unit C on page 63; note that the leaves in the setting block are not divided as they are in the block.

Quilt Assembly and Finishing

1. Sew 3 blocks and 4 sashing strips together to make a row. Press seams toward the sashing. Repeat to make 4 rows.

2. Sew 4 setting blocks and 3 sashing strips together to make a row. Repeat to make 5 rows.

3. Sew alternate rows of blocks and rows of setting blocks together, beginning and ending with a row of setting blocks.

4. Measure the length and width of the quilt top through the center. The quilt should measure approximately 35" x 46". Piece 4"-wide strips of varying lengths of assorted red fabrics together to outside measurements of quilt to make border strips for each side of quilt.

5. Referring to "Borders with Corner Squares" on page 12, measure, trim, and sew the border strips to the side edges of the quilt top first, and then to the top and bottom edges.

6. Layer the quilt top, batting, and backing; then baste. Quilt as desired.

7. Bind the edges of the quilt and add a label.

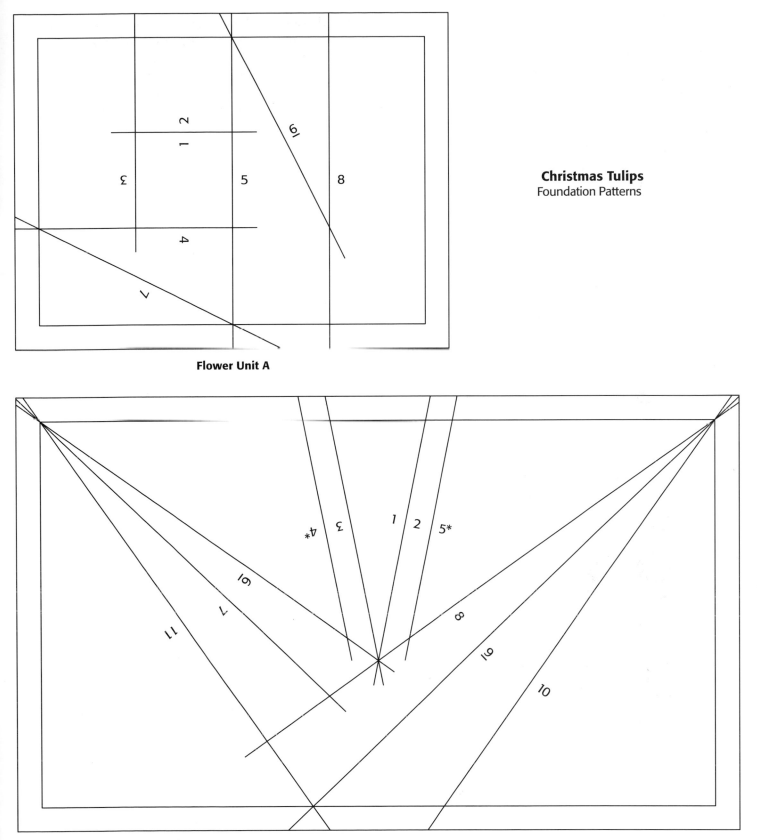

Christmas Tulips
Foundation Patterns

Flower Unit A

Leaf Unit C

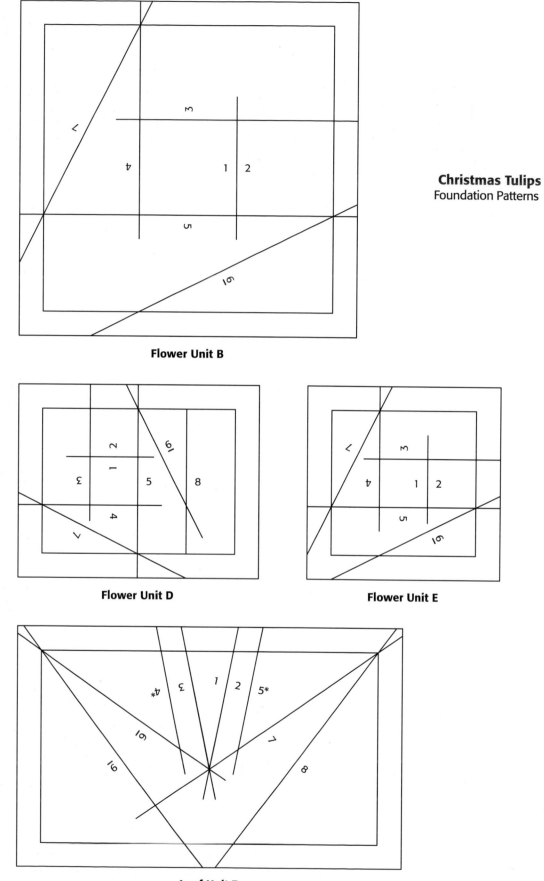

Christmas Tulips
Foundation Patterns

Flower Unit B

Flower Unit D

Flower Unit E

Leaf Unit F

Christmas Stocking

Christmas Stocking by Jenni Paige, 2000, Meridian, Idaho, 26½" x 30½".

This is an easy project to make, even in the hustle and bustle of December!
The pocket in the top of the stocking can be filled with favorite Christmas
cards, candy canes, or special treats for holiday visitors.

Materials: *42"-wide fabric*

1 yd. tan for border base, background, and corner squares

¼ yd. each of 4 or 5 purple, green, and red fabrics for border strips

2 fat quarters or ⅝ yd. purple for stocking

1 fat quarter gold for stocking

¼ yd. red for cuff, toe, and heel

Scraps of green for holly leaves

Scraps of red for holly berries

1 yd. for backing

⅜ yd. for binding

31" x 35" piece of batting

505 spray adhesive (optional)

Freezer paper

Cutting

From tan background fabric, cut:

> 1 piece, 18" x 25", for border base
>
> 1 piece, 20" x 25", for background
>
> 4 squares, 4" x 4", for corner squares

From each border fabric, cut:

> 2 or 3 strips, each 18" long x random widths (1½", 2", 2½")

From the binding fabric, cut:

> 4 strips, 2" x 42"

Construct Background

1. Place the border base fabric on your work surface. Arrange the border strips across the base fabric so it is completely covered; secure the strips in place with pins or spray adhesive.

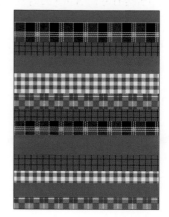

2. Stitch the border strips in place ¼" from the raw edges using a short stitch length (12–13 stitches per inch).

3. Cut the striped border fabric you have just created into four border strips, each 4" x 25". Join border strips to the sides of the background rectangle, *wrong sides together,* so the seam allowances are on the front of the quilt top.

4. Trim the 2 remaining border strips to 4" x 20". Sew one 4" corner square to each end of the remaining 2 border strips, *wrong sides together.* Sew border strips, *wrong sides together,* to the top and bottom edges of the quilt top.

5. Layer the quilt top, batting, and backing; then baste. Machine-quilt in a random allover design. Trim the batting and backing to square up the quilt top.

6. Bind the edges and add a label.

Construct the Stocking

1. Cut a 20" x 11" piece of freezer paper. Trace the stocking template pattern on page 69 onto the non-shiny side, adding a 7¼" x 10½" rectangle to the top of the pattern above the dashed line.

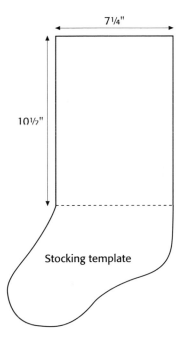

Stocking template

2. Cut 2 pieces of purple fabric and one piece of gold fabric slightly larger than stocking template. Layer the 3 stocking fabrics (1 gold between 2 purple), right sides up. Lay the freezer-paper stocking template shiny side down on the fabric stack, and press with a hot, dry iron. Pin the layers together. Cut exactly along the edge of the template.

3. Remove the freezer-paper template and secure the stocking layers together with more pins or spray adhesive.

4. Trace the toe and heel template patterns onto freezer paper and cut out. Place the freezer-paper templates on the right side of the toe and heel fabric; press with an iron. Cut out 1 toe and 1 heel. Remove the freezer-paper template. Pin the toe and heel to the stocking as indicated on the stocking template.

5. Stitch the toe and heel pieces in place ¼" from the edges, and then again ¼" inside the first row of stitching. Continue stitching rows spaced ¼" apart, filling in toe and heel as indicated on template.

6. Trace 8 star templates onto freezer paper and cut out. Arrange the freezer-paper stars on the stocking. Press in place with an iron.

7. Stitch around the outer edges of the star templates using a short stitch length (12–13 stitches per inch); do not catch the freezer paper in your stitches.

8. Remove the freezer-paper stars. With small, sharp scissors, carefully cut through the center of a star through the top purple layer of the stocking, exposing the gold layer underneath. Cut inside the star outline, leaving a ⅛" seam allowance inside the star stitching. Repeat for the remaining stars.

9. Carefully cut between the lines of stitching on the toe and heel, cutting through the red and top purple layers of fabric.

Appliqué

1. Place the quilted top on your work surface. Place the stocking in the center of the quilt top, allowing room at the upper edge of the stocking for the cuff. Stitch the stocking to the quilt top ¼" from the raw edges, using a short stitch length and leaving the top unstitched.

2. Trace the stocking-cuff template pattern onto freezer paper and cut out. Press the template onto the right side of the red cuff fabric; layer on a second piece of cuff fabric. Cut around the outer edges of the template. Remove the freezer paper. Stitch the 2 cuff pieces together, ¼" from the raw edges.

3. Pin the cuff to the stocking, overlapping the top of the stocking by about 2". Stitch in place, leaving the top open where indicated.

4. Trace 8 holly leaves and 6 berries onto freezer paper using the template patterns on page 69. Layer 2 pieces of leaf fabric. Press the 8 leaf templates onto the top layer of leaf fabric; secure layers together with pins or spray adhesive. Cut around the 8 leaf templates to cut a total of 16 leaves. Layer 2 pieces of berry fabric. Press 6 berry templates onto the fabric; secure layers together. Cut around the 6 templates to cut a total of 12 berries.

5. Layer 2 leaves together to make 8 sets. Place 2 leaf sets and 3 berries on each corner square and secure in place. Stitch ⅛" from the raw edges.

6. Wash the finished quilt in a washing machine with warm soapy water. Dry thoroughly in a clothes dryer. Trim excess threads; press with an iron if necessary.

7. Fill the stocking with candy canes and Christmas cards.

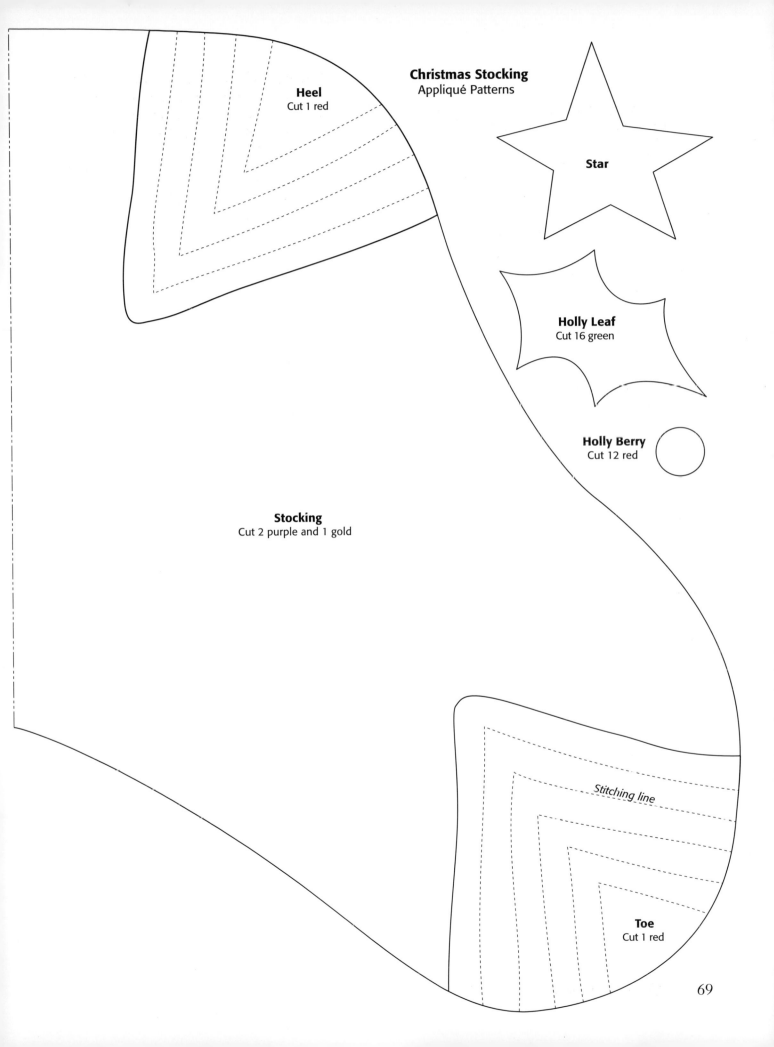

Heel
Cut 1 red

Christmas Stocking
Appliqué Patterns

Star

Holly Leaf
Cut 16 green

Holly Berry
Cut 12 red

Stocking
Cut 2 purple and 1 gold

Stitching line

Toe
Cut 1 red

69

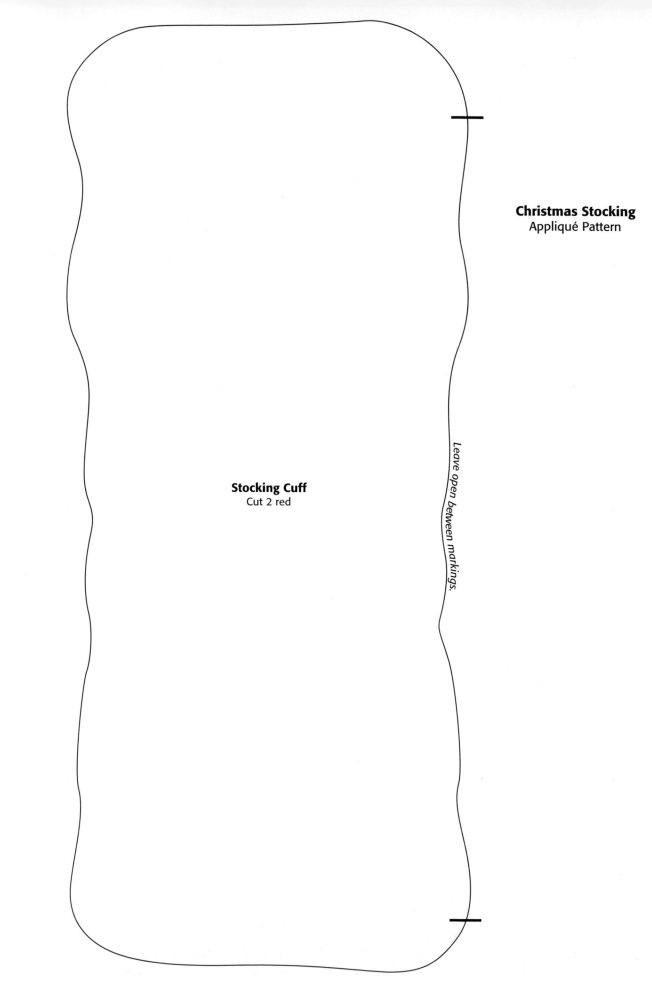

Christmas Stocking
Appliqué Pattern

Stocking Cuff
Cut 2 red

Leave open between markings.

Holiday Reflections

Holiday Reflections by Retta Warehime, 2000, Kennewick, Washington, 48" x 64".
Machine quilted by Pam Clarke.

One of Retta's early quilt designs, "Crystal Reflections," inspired this quilt. She updated the design by adding stars and using traditional Christmas colors.

Materials: *42"-wide fabric*

1⅝ yds. green for blocks, border, and binding

3 yds. for background

1⅓ yds. red for blocks and border

3 yds. for backing

52" x 68" piece of batting

Cutting

From the green fabric, cut:

6 strips, 2½" x 42"; crosscut 2 strips into 48 strips, 1½" x 2½", for blocks and border

3 strips, 4½" x 42"; crosscut into 24 squares, 4½" x 4½", for blocks and border

2 strips, 7½" x 10", for blocks and border

6 strips, 2" x 42", for binding

From the background fabric, cut:

11 strips, 4½" x 42"; crosscut 5 strips into 124 strips, 2½" x 4½", for blocks and border

6 strips, 2½" x 42"; crosscut into 96 squares, 2½" x 2½", for blocks and border

10 strips, 1½" x 42"; crosscut into 256 squares, 1½" x 1½", for blocks and border

6 strips, 7½" x 10", for blocks and border

From the red fabric, cut:

7 strips, 2½" x 42"; crosscut 3 strips into 80 strips, 1½" x 2½", for blocks and border

3 strips, 4½" x 42"; crosscut into 24 squares, 4½" x 4½", for blocks and border

4 strips, 7½" x 10", for blocks and border

Assemble Units

1. Sew one 2½" x 42" green strip to one 4½" x 42" background strip to make a strip set. Repeat for 2 more strip sets. From the strip sets, cut 48 units 2½" wide (Unit #1).

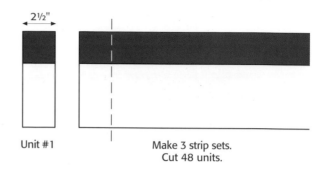

Unit #1   Make 3 strip sets.
          Cut 48 units.

2. Sew one 2½" x 42" red strip to one 4½" x 42" background strip to make a strip set. Repeat for 2 more strip sets. From the strip sets, cut 48 units 2½" wide (Unit #2).

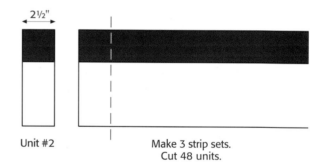

Unit #2   Make 3 strip sets.
          Cut 48 units.

3. Sew one 2½" x 42" red strip to one 2½" x 42" green strip, right sides together. From the strip set, cut 14 units 2½" wide (Unit #3). Set aside for outer border.

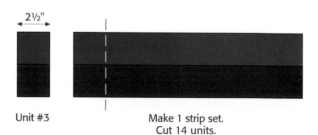

Unit #3   Make 1 strip set.
          Cut 14 units.

4. Using a ruler and soft-leaded pencil, draw a diagonal line from corner to corner on the back of the 2½" x 2½" background squares.

5. Align one 2½" x 2½" background square with one corner of a 4½" green square. Stitch along the diagonal line. Trim ¼" from the stitching line; press seam allowances toward the background fabric. Repeat on the opposite corner of the 4½" green square to make Unit #4. Repeat to make 24 units from green squares. Repeat with 4½" red squares to make 24 red units (Unit #5).

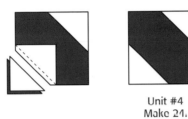

Unit #4
Make 24.

Unit #5
Make 24.

6. Using a ruler and soft-leaded pencil, draw a diagonal line from corner to corner on the back of 112 of the 1½" x 1½" background squares.

7. Position a 1½" background square on one end of a 1½" x 2½" green piece. Stitch along the diagonal line. Trim ¼" from the stitching line; press seam allowances toward the background fabric to make Unit A. Repeat to make 48 green units. Repeat with 1½" x 2½" red strips. Make 80 red units (Unit B).

Unit A
Make 48.

Unit B
Make 80.

8. Using a fine-point permanent-ink marker, draw a 2½" square grid, 4 across and 3 down, on each 7½" x 10" background piece. Draw a diagonal line through each square. Layer a background piece over each of 2 green and 4 red 7½" x 10" pieces. Sew ¼" to each side of the marked diagonal lines. Cut on all marked lines to yield 48 green bias squares and 96 red bias squares. Square-up 80 red bias squares to 1½".

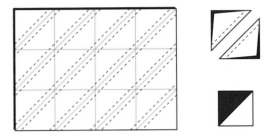

9. Sew one 1½" background square to each of the 1½" bias squares. The green units are Unit C and the red units are Unit D.

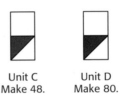

Unit C
Make 48.

Unit D
Make 80.

10. Sew one A unit to one C unit to make Unit #6. Repeat to make 48 units.

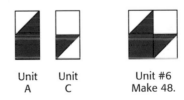

Unit
A

Unit
C

Unit #6
Make 48.

11. Sew one B unit to one D unit to make Unit #7. Repeat to make 80 units.

Unit
B

Unit
D

Unit #7
Make 80.

Block Assembly

Piece 24 green blocks and 24 red blocks as shown.

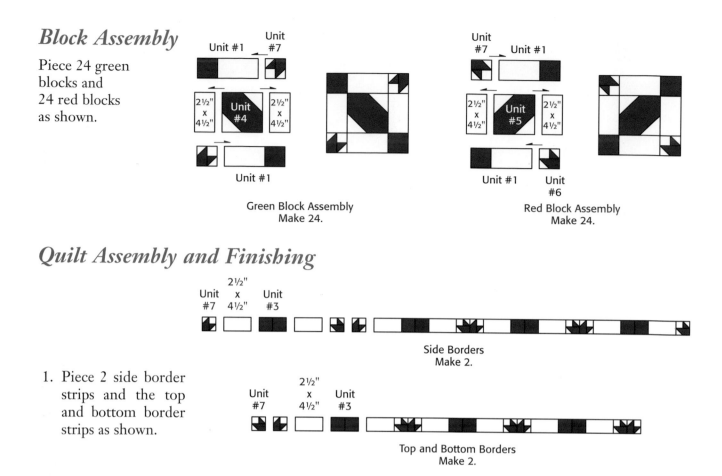

Green Block Assembly
Make 24.

Red Block Assembly
Make 24.

Quilt Assembly and Finishing

Side Borders
Make 2.

1. Piece 2 side border strips and the top and bottom border strips as shown.

Top and Bottom Borders
Make 2.

2. Arrange the blocks in 8 rows of 6 blocks each as shown. Sew the blocks together in horizontal rows. Press the seam allowances in opposite directions from row to row.

3. Join the rows together.

4. Referring to "Straight-Cut Borders" on page 12, sew the border strips from step 1 to the side edges of the quilt top and then to the top and bottom edges.

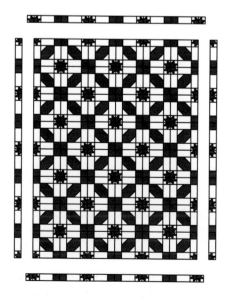

5. Layer the quilt top, batting, and backing; then baste. Quilt as desired.

6. Bind the edges and add a label.

Ruth's Bouquet

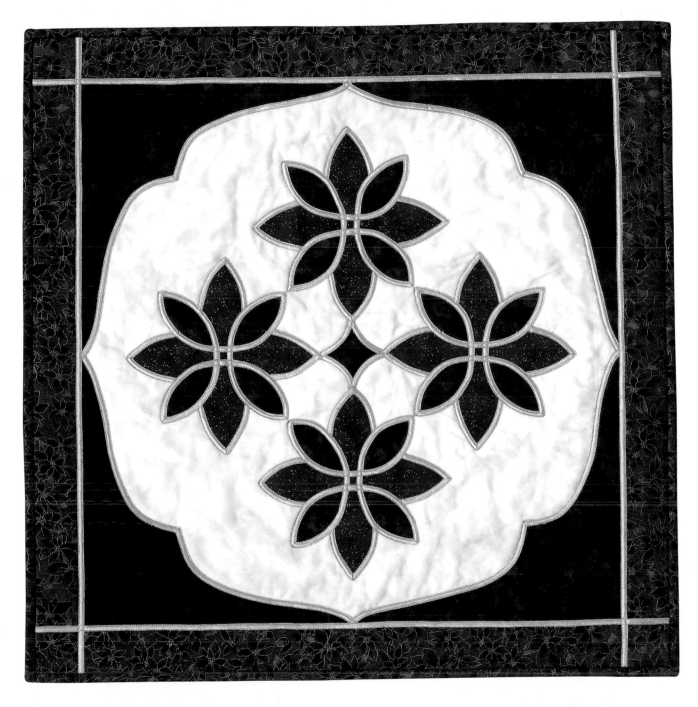

Ruth's Bouquet by Gretchen Hudock, 2000, Slinger, Wisconsin, 24" x 24".

Gretchen's mother carried poinsettias at her holiday wedding on January 5, 1946. Gretchen's father had just returned from the war, and the church was still decorated for Christmas. Gretchen made this quilt for her parents, who celebrated fifty-five years together in 2001.

Materials: *42"-wide fabric*

¾ yd. for background

¼ yd. or 1 fat quarter red, for poinsettia

⅓ yd. green, for poinsettia, center piece, and corner pieces

¼ yd. print for border

¼ yd. for binding

⅞ yd. for backing

26" x 26" piece of batting

1¼ yds. fusible web

1 roll (11 yards) fusible ¼" bias tape

Cutting:

From background fabric, cut:

1 square, 24" x 24"

From the binding fabric, cut:

5 strips, 2" x 42"

Block Assembly

1. Fold background square diagonally from corner to corner; press lightly. Repeat in opposite direction. Mark a line 2" in from all cut edges, using a fabric pencil, to create a 20" square on the background fabric.

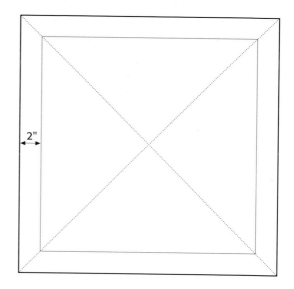

2. Transfer the pattern on page 79 to paper. Lay background fabric over pattern, matching fold lines with lines on pattern, and tape over a light box or sunny window. Trace design onto fabric with fabric marking pencil or pen. Repeat in each section to trace a total of 4 designs. Set aside.

3. Trace the poinsettia, leaf, and center template patterns on page 78 onto the paper side of the fusible web according to the number needed. Referring to "Fusible Appliqué" on page 10, prepare the appliqué pieces and appliqué them to the background fabric.

4. Fuse a 6" x 42" piece of fusible web to the back of the border fabric. Cut into 2 strips measuring 2" x 20" and 2 strips measuring 2" x 24". Fuse to the outer edges of the quilt, aligning inner edges to the marked lines. Prepare the corner appliqué pieces, referring to "Fusible Appliqué" on page 10 (see pattern on page 78). Place corner pieces into position, inside fused border strips, as shown in the photo on page 75. Fuse into place.

Finishing

1. Layer the fused quilt top, batting, and backing; pin baste.

2. Apply fusible bias tape to each side of center diamond, beginning and ending strips at tips of flowers; the raw edges will be covered when the flowers are edged. Stitch close to the edges of the strips with a stitch length of 15 stitches per inch.

3. Apply fusible bias tape to each flower petal from X to X as indicated on the pattern on page 79, mitering the strip at the petal tip and leaving a ¼" extension on each end. This will be trimmed after leaf sections are edged. Stitch close to the edges of the strips.

4. Apply fusible bias to leaf sections starting at point Y and continue around each leaf to return to point Y; miter bias at the leaf tips. Tuck ending tail under crosspiece at point Y. Stitch close to edges of strips.

5. Apply fusible bias to inner edges of corner pieces. Stitch close to edges of strips. Apply fusible bias to inner edges of border. Stitch close to edges of strips.

6. Remove basting pins. Trim edges of backing and batting even with quilt top.

7. Bind the edges of the quilt and add a label.

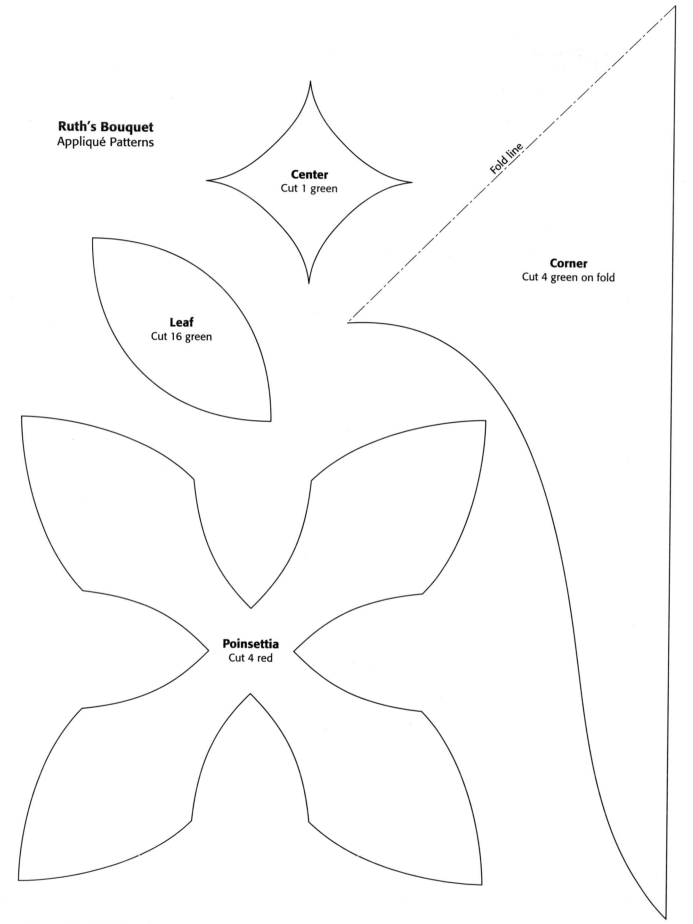

Ruth's Bouquet
Appliqué Patterns

Center
Cut 1 green

Fold line

Corner
Cut 4 green on fold

Leaf
Cut 16 green

Poinsettia
Cut 4 red

Ruth's Bouquet
Tracing Pattern

X X

Y

Diagonal fold line

Diagonal fold line

North Wind

North Wind by Tricia Lund, 2000, Seattle, Washington, 44½" x 56½".
Hand quilted by Hazel Montague.

What better way to warm up when north winds howl than by snuggling under this friendly quilt? The limited color palette creates a rich, antique look.

Finished Block Size: 6" x 6"

Materials: *42"-wide fabric*

2¾ yds. assorted light prints and plaids for blocks

2¾ yds. assorted dark prints and plaids for blocks

1⅝ yds. black print for border

⅝ yd. for binding if cut on the bias, or ⅜ yd. if cut on the crosswise grain

3 yds. for backing

49" x 61" piece of batting

Cutting

From the assorted light prints and plaids, cut:

> 24 squares, 4⅞" x 4⅞"; cut squares once diagonally to make 48 triangles for blocks
>
> 21 strips, 3" x 42", for foundation piecing

From the assorted dark prints and plaids, cut:

> 24 squares, 4⅞" x 4⅞"; cut squares once diagonally to make 48 triangles for blocks
>
> 21 strips, 3" x 42", for foundation piecing

From the black print, cut:

> 2 strips, 4½" x 51", for side borders
>
> 2 strips, 4½" x 46", for top and bottom borders

From the binding fabric, cut:

> 2"-wide bias strips to total 217" or cut 6 strips, 2" x 42", on the crosswise grain

General Foundation Piecing Guidelines

1. The unit that you place under the presser foot consists of 3 layers: the paper foundation (with the marked side up) on top and 2 layers of fabric, right sides together, beneath the paper.

2. Use 12–15 stitches per inch to anchor the stitches well. Backstitch at the ends of sewing lines. If you make a mistake and have to take out a seam, put a piece of tape over the perforated seam on the marked side of the paper.

3. The sewing sequence is numbered on the foundation. Be sure to rotate the foundation so that the numbers are right side up as you sew the unit.

4. If you are not sure if the next fabric piece will cover its allotted space, place a pin along the sewing line instead of sewing and open the piece to see if it fits. If necessary, adjust and test again. An asterisk on the foundation indicates that you should take extra care to see that the piece will fit.

5. Do not remove the paper foundation until you are ready to sew the units into blocks. This helps prevent the distortion that can be caused by handling.

6. The finished unit is a mirror image of the foundation. For example, the triangle on the left side of the paper foundation will be on the right side of the finished block.

Pattern Preparation

Make 48 copies of the foundation patterns on page 84. Cut each unit apart ⅛" to ¼" outside the cutting line.

Block Assembly

1. Place a 3" light strip and a 3" dark strip right sides together. With the marked side of the pattern up, place the fabrics beneath position 1, with the dark fabric against the paper and the edges of the strips extending ¼" into position 2.

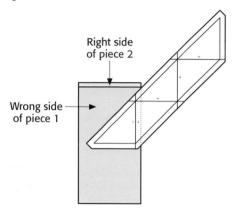

Right side of piece 2

Wrong side of piece 1

2. Hold the fabrics in position and place the unit under the presser foot, paper side up. Sew along the line between positions 1 and 2 through the paper and both layers of fabric.

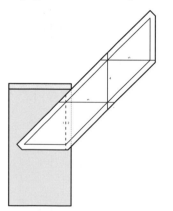

3. Trim excess strips just beyond the foundation edge. Fold back the light fabric over position 2 and press.

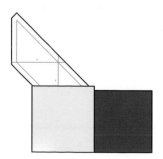

4. Place a dark 3" strip right sides together over the fabrics in positions 1 and 2. Sew along the line between positions 2 and 3. Trim excess from strip and trim seam allowances to ¼". Fold piece back and press.

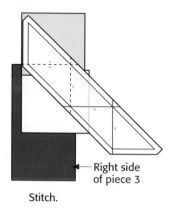

Right side of piece 3

Stitch.

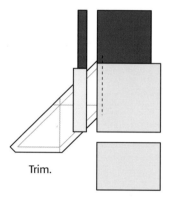

Trim.

Press.

5. Continue to add strips of fabric, alternating light and dark strips between subsequent positions. Trim and press after adding each fabric. When the foundation is complete, trim along the outside cutting line. Make 48 foundation-pieced units, beginning and ending with dark fabric.

Make 48.

6. Construct 48 foundation-pieced units, beginning and ending with light fabric.

Make 48.

7. Join a dark triangle to a dark foundation-pieced unit. Repeat for all 48 units. Join a light triangle to a light foundation-pieced unit. Repeat for all 48 units.

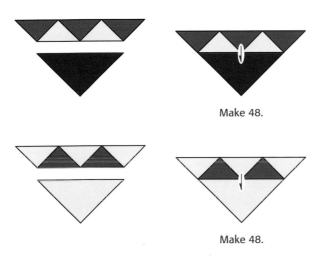

Make 48.

Make 48.

8. Join a light foundation-pieced and a dark foundation-pieced unit to make a block.

Quilt Assembly and Finishing

1. Arrange the blocks into 8 rows of 6 blocks each. Join the blocks into horizontal rows. Join the rows.

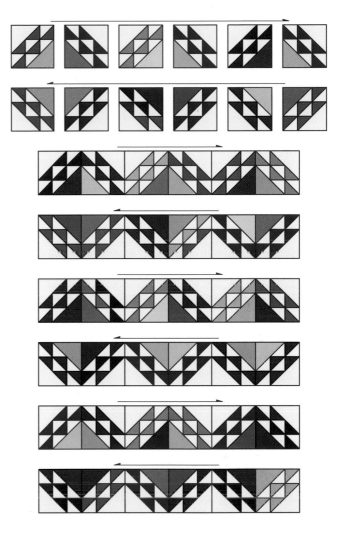

2. Referring to "Straight-Cut Borders" on page 12, measure, trim, and sew the border strips to the sides of the quilt top first, and then to the top and bottom edges.

3. Layer the quilt top, batting, and backing; then baste. Quilt as desired.

4. Bind the edges of the quilt and add a label.

North Wind
Foundation Patterns

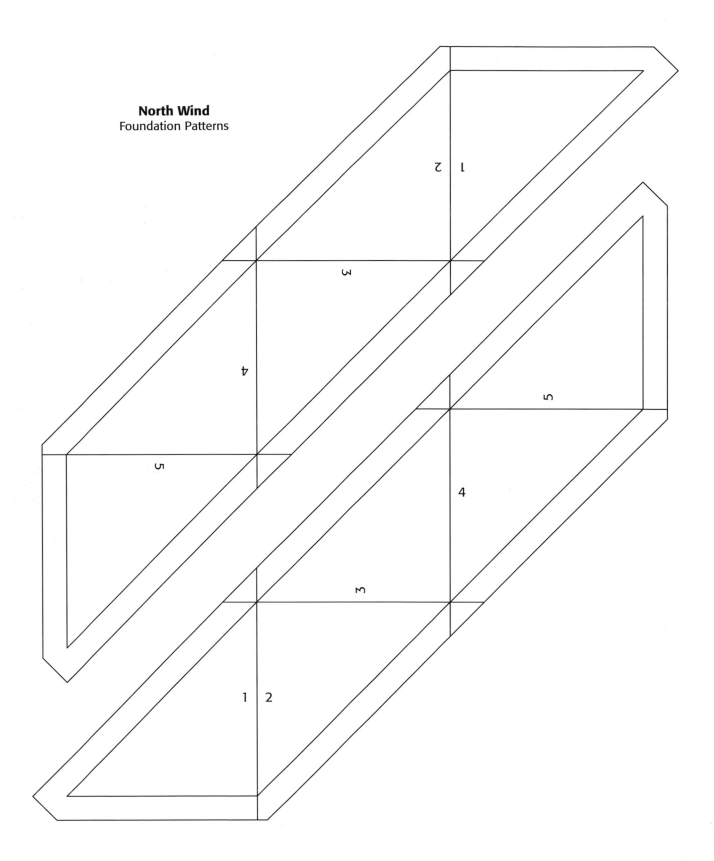

Cardinals

Cardinals by Deborah J. Moffett-Hall, 2000, Hatfield, Pennsylvania, 23" x 39½".

Deb loves to decorate for the holidays, spending hours to get everything just right. When friends say that her home is warm and inviting, her husband laughs, points to the holiday quilts on the walls and draped over every chair and sofa, and says, "Of course it's warm; the whole house is wrapped in a quilt!"

Materials: *42"-wide fabric*

¼ yd. medium red for berries

¼ yd. dark red for cardinals and berries

1⅛ yds. dark blue for quilt center, outer border, and backing

⅜ yd. light blue for quilt center

⅜ yd. light red for cardinals

⅛ yd. or scraps of white for snow

⅛ yd. or scraps of yellow for beaks and feet

⅛ yd. or scraps of black for cardinal faces

⅛ yd. light green #1 for quilt-center leaves

¼ yd. dark green #1 for quilt-center leaves

¼ yd. light green #2 for inner-border leaves

¼ yd. dark green #2 for inner-border leaves

½ yd. gold for inner border

⅜ yd. navy blue for binding

27" x 44" piece of thin batting

¼ yd. heavy fusible web for attaching berries

Cutting

From the dark red fabric, cut:

   1 strip, 2" x 42"; crosscut into 15 squares, 2" x 2", for cardinals

   1 strip, 1¼" x 42"; crosscut into 6 squares, 1¼" x 1¼", for cardinals

From the dark blue fabric, cut:

   11 strips, 2" x 42"; crosscut into 2 strips, 2" x 36½", for the outer border; 2 strips, 2" x 23", for the outer border; 59 squares, 2" x 2", for the quilt center

   1 strip, 1¼" x 10"; crosscut into 6 squares, 1¼" x 1¼", for quilt center

From the light blue fabric, cut:

   3 strips, 2" x 42"; crosscut into 58 squares, 2" x 2", for quilt center

   1 strip, 1¼" x 5"; crosscut into 3 squares, 1¼" x 1¼", for quilt center

From the light red fabric, cut:

   3 strips, 2" x 42"; crosscut into 49 squares 2" x 2", for cardinals

   1 strip, 1¼" x 14"; crosscut into 9 squares, 1¼" x 1¼", for cardinals

From the white fabric, cut:

   1 strip 2" x 42"; crosscut into 17 squares, 2" x 2", for snow

From the yellow fabric, cut:

   1 strip, 1¼" x 10"; crosscut into 6 squares, 1¼" x 1¼", for beaks and feet

From the black fabric, cut:

   1 strip, 2" x 5"; crosscut into 2 squares, 2" x 2", for cardinal faces

   1 strip, 1¼" x 3"; crosscut into 2 squares, 1¼" x 1¼", for cardinal faces

From the light green #1 fabric, cut:

   1 strip, 2" x 42"; crosscut into 18 squares, 2" x 2", for quilt-center leaves

   1 square, 1¼" x 1¼", for quilt-center leaves

From the dark green #1 fabric, cut:

   2 strips, 2" x 42"; crosscut into 35 squares, 2" x 2", for quilt-center leaves

   1 strip 1¼" x 7"; crosscut into 3 squares, 1¼" x 1¼", for quilt-center leaves

From the light green #2 fabric, cut:

   2 strips, 2" x 42"; crosscut into 36 squares, 2" x 2", for inner-border leaves

   1 strip, 1¼" x 18"; crosscut into 12 squares, 1¼" x 1¼", for inner-border leaves

From the dark green #2 fabric, cut:

   2 strips, 2" x 42"; crosscut into 36 squares 2" x 2", for inner-border leaves

   1 strip, 1¼" x 18"; crosscut into 12 squares 1¼" x 1¼", for inner-border leaves

From the gold fabric, cut:

    4 strips, 2" x 42"; crosscut into 72 squares, 2" x 2", for inner border

    1 strip, 1¼" x 42"; crosscut into 24 squares, 1¼" x 1¼", for inner border

    1 strip, 3½" x 42"; crosscut into 6 squares, 3½" x 3½", for inner border; 6 rectangles, 3½" x 2½", for inner border

From the navy blue fabric, cut:

    4 strips, 2" x 42", for binding

Preparing Appliqués

1. Trace 21 berries close together onto the paper side of the fusible web using the Berry template pattern (page 89). Cut out the group of berries and fuse the web to the wrong side of the medium red fabric, referring to "Fusible Appliqué" on page 10. Cut out the berries and set aside.

2. Trace 17 berries close together onto the paper side of the fusible web using the Berry template pattern. Cut out the group of berries and fuse them to the wrong side of the dark red fabric. Cut out the berries and set them aside.

Sewing the Units

Referring to the diagram above, make pieced bias squares and corner-tip squares from the fabrics indicated, following the instructions below.

Bias squares

1. Place two 2" squares of the desired colors right sides together, with the edges and corners aligned. Using a ruler and soft-leaded pencil, draw a diagonal line from corner to corner on one of the fabrics.

2. Stitch 1 or 2 threads to the side of the marked line. If you stitch on the line, the resulting unit will be slightly smaller than 2" square.

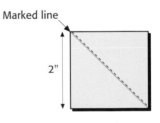

3. Trim ¼" from the stitching on the smaller half of the unit. Press the seam allowances toward the darker fabric.

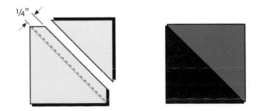

Note: You may find quilt assembly easier if you press intersecting bias squares in opposite directions, regardless of the light or dark side, so the seams match smoothly.

Corner Tips

1. Place a 1¼" square on the upper-right corner of a 2" square, right sides together, with edges and corner aligned. Using a ruler and soft-leaded pencil, draw a diagonal line from corner to corner on the 1¼" square.

2. Stitch 1 or 2 threads to the right of the marked line, on the side closest to the outer corner. If you stitch directly on the marked line, the resulting unit will be smaller than 2" square.

3. Trim ¼" from the stitching on the smaller half of the unit. Press the seam allowances toward the larger square.

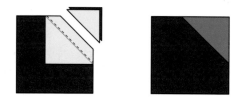

Quilt Assembly and Finishing

1. Lay out the squares for the quilt top as shown in the chart on page 89. Sew the squares into horizontal rows. Press the seam allowances in each row in opposite directions.

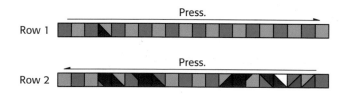

2. Lay the completed rows, in the correct order, on your work surface. Again, check the placement of the squares, bias squares, and corner-tip squares. Place the rows right sides together and pin the block intersections carefully. Sew rows 1 and 2 together. Press the seam up or down, depending on the direction it wants to go.

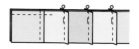

3. Sew rows 3 and 4 together. Check the rows against the chart. Sew together the two-row units from steps 2 and 3, matching the seams carefully. Press the seam up or down. Continue in this manner until all rows are stitched together.

4. Assemble an inner-border segment as shown; press. Repeat to make 12 inner border segments.

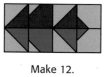

Make 12.

5. Join 4 inner border segments, one 3½" gold square, and two 2" x 3½" gold rectangles, alternating border segments as shown. Repeat to make a top and bottom inner border strip.

Make 2.

6. Join 2 border segments, two 3½" gold squares, and one 2" x 3½" gold rectangle, alternating border segments as shown. Repeat to make 2 side inner border strips.

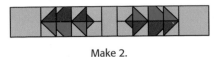

Make 2.

7. Sew the top and bottom pieced inner-border strips to the top and bottom edges of the quilt top, matching the seam intersections; press seams toward the border. Sew the pieced side inner-border strips to the side edges of the quilt top; press the seams toward the border.

8. Referring to "Straight-Cut Borders" on page 12, measure, trim, and sew the outer border strips to the top and bottom edges of the quilt top first, and then to the side edges.

9. Fuse the medium and dark red berries to the quilt top as shown below, following the instructions for "Fusible Appliqué" on page 10.

10. Layer the quilt top, batting, and backing; then baste. Quilt as desired.

11. Bind the edges of the quilt and add a label.

Berry
Cut 21 medium red
and 17 dark red

Christmas Snowflakes

Christmas Snowflakes by Roxanne Carter, 2000, Mukilteo, Washington, 53" x 70".

This sparkling quilt is fun to make and offers a great way to use your fabric stash. If you like, make each snowflake block from a different print.

Finished Quilt Size— Lap Quilt: 53" x 70"
Full: 70" x 88"
Queen/King: 88" x 105"
Finished Block Size—Sister's Choice Block: 8¾"
Alternate Block: 8¾"

Materials: *42"-wide fabric*

Lap quilt

1¾ yds. total or 6 fat quarters print fabrics for Sister's Choice blocks

1¼ yds. background fabric for Sister's Choice blocks

1¾ yds. green print for alternate block, border, and binding

2¼ yds. white print for alternate block and border

3¾ yds. for backing

57" x 74" piece of batting

Full quilt

2⅝ yds. total or 11 fat quarters print fabrics for Sister's Choice blocks

2 yds. background fabric for Sister's Choice blocks

2¼ yds. green print for alternate block, border, and binding

3 yds. white print for alternate block and border

4½ yds. for backing

74" x 92" piece of batting

Queen/king quilt

3 yds. or 17 fat quarters print fabrics for Sister's Choice blocks

2⅞ yds. background fabric for Sister's Choice blocks

3¼ yds. green print for alternate block, border, and binding

3¾ yds. white print for alternate block and border

8 yds. for backing

92" x 109" piece of batting

Cutting:

Lap quilt

For each Sister's Choice block, cut from 1 printed fabric:

9 squares, 2¼" x 2¼"

4 squares, 2⅝" x 2⅝"; cut squares once diagonally to make 8 triangles

Note: Cut pieces for 18 blocks.

From the background fabric, cut:

9 strips, 2¼" x 42"; crosscut into 144 squares, 2¼" x 2¼", for Sister's Choice blocks

6 strips 2⅝" x 42"; crosscut into 72 squares, 2⅝" x 2⅝"; cut once diagonally to make 144 triangles for Sister's Choice blocks

From the green print, cut:

3 strips, 10" x 42"; crosscut into 12 squares, 10" x 10"; cut squares twice diagonally to make 48 triangles for alternate blocks

7 strips, 2½" x 42", for binding

From the white print, cut:

3 strips, 10" x 42"; crosscut into 9 squares, 10" x 10"; cut squares twice diagonally to make 36 triangles for alternate blocks

5 strips, 4⅞" x 42"; crosscut into 10 segments, 4⅞" x 18¾", for border

1 strip, 9¾" x 42"; crosscut into 2 squares, 9¾" x 9¾"; cut once diagonally to make 4 triangles for border

Full quilt

For each Sister's Choice block, cut from 1 printed fabric:

9 squares, 2¼" x 2¼"

4 squares, 2⅝" x 2⅝"; cut squares once diagonally to make 8 triangles

Note: Cut pieces for 32 blocks.

From the background fabric, cut:

16 strips, 2¼" x 42"; crosscut into 256 squares, 2¼" x 2¼", for Sister's Choice blocks

10 strips, 2⅝" x 42"; crosscut into 128 squares, 2⅝" x 2⅝"; cut once diagonally to make 256 triangles for Sister's Choice blocks

From the green print, cut:

5 strips, 10" x 42"; crosscut into 20 squares, 10" x 10"; cut squares twice diagonally to make 80 triangles for alternate blocks

8 strips, 2½" x 42", for binding

From the white print, cut:

4 strips, 10" x 42"; crosscut into 16 squares, 10" x 10"; cut squares twice diagonally to make 64 triangles for alternate blocks

7 strips, 4⅞" x 42"; crosscut into 14 segments, 4⅞" x 18¾", for border

1 strip, 9¾" x 42"; crosscut into 2 squares, 9¾" x 9¾"; cut once diagonally to make 4 triangles for border

Queen/king quilt

For each Sister's Choice block, cut from 1 printed fabric:

9 squares, 2¼" x 2¼"

4 squares, 2⅝" x 2⅝"; cut squares once diagonally to make 8 triangles

Note: Cut pieces for 50 blocks.

From the background fabric, cut:

24 strips, 2¼" x 42"; crosscut into 400 squares, 2¼" x 2¼", for Sister's Choice blocks

15 strips 2⅝" x 42"; crosscut into 200 squares, 2⅝" x 2⅝"; cut once diagonally to make 400 triangles for Sister's Choice blocks

From the green print, cut:

8 strips, 10" x 42"; crosscut into 30 squares, 10" x 10"; cut squares twice diagonally to make 120 triangles for alternate blocks

10 strips, 2½" x 42", for binding

From the white print, cut:

7 strips, 10" x 42"; crosscut into 25 squares, 10" x 10"; cut squares twice diagonally to make 100 triangles for alternate blocks

9 strips, 4⅞" x 42"; crosscut into 18 segments, 4⅞" x 18¾", for border

1 strip, 9¾" x 42"; crosscut into 2 squares, 9¾" x 9¾"; cut once diagonally to make 4 triangles for border

Block Assembly

Sister's Choice Block

1. Join 1 half-square triangle each from the print and background fabrics for the Sister's Choice block.

Make 8.

2. Join a bias square from step 1 to a 2¼" background square. Press seam toward the background fabric.

Make 4.

3. Join a bias square from step 1 to a 2¼" print square. Press seam toward the print fabric.

Make 4.

4. Join the units from steps 2 and 3 together to make the corner unit (Unit A) for the Sister's Choice block.

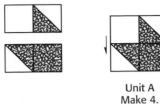

Unit A
Make 4.

5. Join a 2¼" background square and a 2¼" print square. Press seam toward the print square to make Unit B.

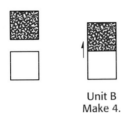

Unit B
Make 4.

6. Join 4 of Unit A, 1 of Unit B, and a 2¼" print square to make a Sister's Choice block, as shown.

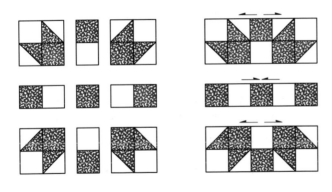

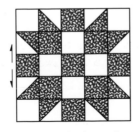

Make 18 for lap quilt.
Make 32 for full quilt.
Make 50 for queen/king quilt.

Alternate Block

Join 2 green-print quarter-square triangles and 2 white-print quarter-square triangles as shown to make an alternate block.

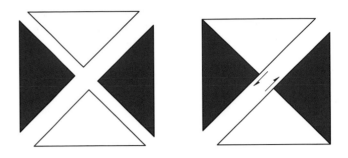

Make 17 for lap quilt.
Make 31 for full quilt.
Make 49 for queen/king quilt.

Border Units

1. Cut the ends of the 4⅞" x 18¾" white-print border segments at 45° angles to make trapezoid pieces.

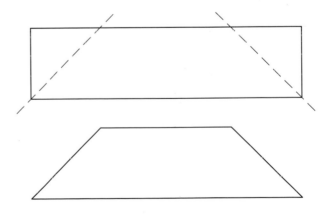

2. Join green-print quarter-square triangles between trapezoid border segments. For the lap quilt, join 3 trapezoids and 4 triangles for the side border strips and 2 trapezoids and 3 triangles for the top and bottom border strips. For the full-size quilt, join 4 trapezoids and 5 triangles for the side border strips and 3 trapezoids and 4 triangles for the top and bottom border strips. For the queen/king-size quilt, join 5 trapezoids and 6 triangles for the side border strips and 4 trapezoids and 5 triangles for the top and bottom border strips.

Quilt Assembly and Finishing

1. Arrange the blocks into rows, alternating the Sister's Choice block and the alternate block. Sew the blocks together in horizontal rows. Press seams toward alternate blocks.

2. Join the rows together. Sew the side border strips to the quilt top, aligning seam lines; then sew the top and bottom border strips to the quilt top. Sew the white-print half-square triangles to the corners of the quilt top.

3. Layer the quilt top, batting, and backing; then baste. Quilt as desired.

4. Bind the edges of the quilt and add a label.

Full size

Queen/king size

Contributors

Roxanne Carter has been a quiltmaker for more than twenty years. Her particular passion involves working with existing designs, devising ways to make them easier to construct. She also enjoys creating new designs. She is the author of three books for That Patchwork Place: *All Star Sampler, Easy Star Sampler,* and *Shortcuts Sampler.* A dedicated and popular quilt instructor for more than eleven years, Roxanne is in such demand that teaching has become a full-time occupation. Roxanne lives in Mukilteo, Washington.

Mimi Dietrich is a renowned appliqué expert and celebrated quiltmaker who simply loves appliquéd quilts. When she's not appliquéing, she's teaching appliqué classes! Mimi lives in Baltimore, Maryland. She is the author of numerous That Patchwork Place books, including *Happy Endings, The Easy Art of Appliqué* (with Roxi Eppler), *Baltimore Bouquets,* and *Pink Ribbon Quilts.* Her books have sold nearly 400,000 copies to date.

Vicki Garnas learned how to sew from her mother and how to quilt from books. She began stenciling quilts after learning the techniques at a quilt-guild meeting. Vicki has developed a simple way to make unusual quilts using common paints, pens, and embellishments. She has shared her techniques in classes, lectures, on *The Carol Duvall Show,* and in her book, *Fast & Fun Stenciled Quilts.* Vicki lives in Granada Hills, California.

Amy Whalen Helmkamp first discovered quilting in 1977 when her mother introduced her to the craft, but she did not become fully immersed in it until many years later. In addition to authoring the book, *Stained Glass Quilts Made Easy,* Amy produces and sells her own line of quilting patterns. She recently appeared on the television program *Kaye Wood's Quilting Friends.* Amy lives in Lake Oswego, Oregon.

Gretchen Kluth Hudock began quilting in 1984 and designing quilts in 1989. She has had a number of patterns published in books and magazines in the years since. Gretchen currently serves as the Quilting Consultant for Nancy's Notions, a job that involves teaching, testing new products, demonstrating, and promoting quilting as much as possible. She especially enjoys helping beginners get a good foundation in quilting. Gretchen lives in Slinger, Wisconsin. She publishes her own line of patterns under the name PineBerry Patch.

Tricia Lund has been a quiltmaker for 25 years. She enjoys both traditional and original designs, and her quilts generally feature a large variety of fabrics with which she obtains a painterly, antique look. Tricia has taught classes in foundation piecing in the US and Canada. She co-authored, with Judy Pollard, *Classic Quilts with Precise Foundation Piecing* (That Patchwork Place), and is currently working on a book of small classic quilts. She lives in Seattle, Washington.

Deb Moffet-Hall has designed and stitched quilts for more than a decade. More than 150 of her projects have appeared in quilting magazines through the years. She has authored two quilt books and contributed several projects to the popular *Quilted for Christmas* series from That Patchwork Place. Deb loves to travel, teach, and lecture on quilts and her new interest, beadwork. She lives in Hatfield, Pennsylvania.

Pam Mostek has loved making pretty things for as long as she can remember. Even as a child she and her mother were always involved in creating some exciting project. It was a natural choice for her to pursue a degree in art and education, and she spent years as a high school art teacher spreading her love of creating. She began quilting about 15 years ago, and it has been her passion ever since. Today she spends her time designing and creating quilts for books and her pattern company, Making Lemonade Designs. Pamela lives in Cheney, Washington.

Jenni Paige began quilting in 1987, working her way through the traditional quilt patterns and quickly developing a love for all things folk art, especially appliqué. She has been a quilt shop owner, a teacher in Idaho and Washington, and a designer. She recently moved back home to Nampa, Idaho, where, with the help of her husband, she started the I Wanna Quilt! Pattern Company, which primarily features her signature Stitch 'n Fray technique.

Judy Pollard loves to quilt! An early fascination with fabric inspired her to learn to sew. Then, in the late 1970s, a quilt store flier led her to a quilting class and a consuming passion for quilting. She especially enjoys designing and piecing. Lately, her life has been filled with projects for friends' babies and weddings, joyous occasions always deserving of a new quilt. Judy is the co-author, with Tricia Lund, of *Classic Quilts with Precise Foundation Piecing* (That Patchwork Place). She lives in Seattle, Washington.

Jean Van Bockel is a quilter and designer who specializes in hand applique designs. She works at a local quilt shop, where she has also taught year-long, block-of-the-month classes in appliqué. Jean lives in Coeur d' Alene, Idaho.

Retta Warehime loves designing and piecing. Wherever she goes, everything she sees brings ideas for new patterns. Retta's mother introduced her to sewing, setting her on a lifelong course of learning, teaching, designing, and creating. Today, she designs patterns for her own business, Sew Cherished. She also designs and is an editor for Fiber Mosaics. Retta lives in Kennewick, Washington.